THE APRON OF HUMILITY

Becoming A Disciple

The Apron of Humility

Becoming A Disciple

PK PRICE

LAURUS BOOKS

The Apron of Humility

Becoming A Disciple

By PK Price

Paperback: ISBN: 978-1-957528-02-1

Mobi-ePub: ISBN: 978-1-957528-03-8

Published by LAURUS BOOKS

DOVE AND APRON ILLUSTRATION BY JEANNE L. MCCOY

LAURUS BOOKS
AN IMPRINT OF THE LAURUS COMPANY, INC.
www.TheLaurusCompany.com

This book may be purchased in paperback from TheLaurusCompany.com, all Amazon sites, and most other online retailers around the world. May also be available in formats for electronic readers from their respective stores. Available to booksellers at Spring Arbor.

The Apron of Humility

Becoming A Disciple

ACKNOWLEDGEMENTS

Mentors and Elders

*L*IFE brings so many colorful people "going our way." These people may touch via a look, a word, a picture, a gift, a correction, a laugh. The stay may be minutes or years, but the commonality is they leave a flavoring in one's life in some manner. Who but God could name them all?

The following I know somewhat intimately because we have walked many years and miles together. Chosen from the traditions of worship: Catholicism, Baptist-ism, and Non-Denominational-ism, these representations of "isms" were God's choicest for one who had early roots in Brethren-ism and Methodism. My heart continues in tenderness toward all, and my gratefulness through praise echoes in the heavenlies. May I be as fruitful as they.

• **Jeannine**, a woman large in stature who oozed love and was extraordinarily deep and pure in Spirit ways and was God's instrument for spiritual director/mother/mentor for twenty-five years and the Elder I was always returned to for confirming guidance. In the beginning and throughout the years because of her intimacy with the Holy Spirit, healing gift, knowledge, wisdom, and discernment, I received a colossal dose of inner healing that spawned hope, stabilized mind, and facilitated a sense of worth that continues to this present day. Jeannine was intimate with the truth and power of "pick up your cross and come follow me." It is a foundational underpinning of truth in my Christian walk that has kept me in times of bewilderment and spiritual fog. My being remains ever full because of her unconditional love, teachings, guidance, and touch upon my life.

• **Warren**, spiritual father, pastor, and overseer who believed and endorsed God's calling on my life with ordination and a sending forth. He is to me the male counterpart to Jeannine. Endowed with great portions of grace and gentleness, it was through Warren that God the Father's vast grace and gentleness began to be experiential. As leader and pastor-shepherd in the multi-cultural house of God, to me he modeled equality, compassion, and freedom of ministerial expression. He imparted wisdom and knowledge concerning the ways of church. Even now, although miles and years of in-house apart, he stands always in my heart singularly as my pastor and as spiritual father.

• **Jeanne** is teacher, nurse, and trusted friend. She is teacher of everything God's Word, teacher of many things physical, and an enduring example of grace and love in action on earth. Her unrelenting hunger, settled understanding, and colorful delivery of His Word continues to be a constant fascination to me. After walking together in ministry for over twenty years here and abroad, we have seen both the excellent and non-excellent of one another. God alone gets tribute for the wonderment of our walking and staying together, for He took two quite different people and caused us to link for His purposes. I esteem Jeanne. She has excelled in love, patience, and graciousness toward me in and out of season. My life continues to be enriched beyond expression in our present day personal and ministerial relationship.

• And I give thanks for **Tim**, Jeanne's husband, who is a man secure in his own calling and who unconditionally has supported and walked together with us in ministry as an Elder and administrator.

• To my **God**, I am grateful for gifting me with exceptional spiritual mentors in **Jeannine**, **Warren**, and **Jeanne**.

Foundations matter. Love matters.
Accountability and eldership matter for sound growth and development.
I am grateful.

PREFACE

On Humility

When I received the title of this book, I was sitting quietly in a friend's car listening to spring birds chirping in a parking area in Brevard, North Carolina. Instantly, I recalled an apron assignment I received in my sewing class as a young teen, which is further spoken about in the Introduction of this book. It has taken the unfolding of these subsequent years of life to consider the duality of the title and to respond to the word *humility*. In 1 Peter 5, we are told to "be clothed with humility." The Greek word literally means *to put on the apron of humility* (Tapeinos). It is the *putting on* that I would like to briefly address.

The command to *put on* suggests it is not a quality of spiritual clothing that is intrinsic naturally to man. And so, it is a fundamental truth encompassing all of humanity that humility, or a humbleness, is an attribute, a mindset, a quality, a way that is attained, not ascribed to us by our Creator genetically, philosophically, or surgically. Appointed to a lofty position, or titled within the house of God or in the marketplace does not dress one with humility. The way of humility God has ordained is by no other means than prostrating one's whole personhood before Him first and then all others. It is choice of will. It is choice of desire. It is a lifelong choice of putting on. The war between humility and pride began in the heavenlies between the Creator and the created when the most splendid created being ever, though non-human, chose a mission and lifestyle to self-exalt. It repeated itself in the Garden of Eden when man chose his way over God's way and as though in a trifecta race man on earth continues the same natural pattern of pride and superiority over the unnatural subjugation of self.

And so God prescribed the only antidote for His beloved: Humility. It is a Christ-likeness that can be ours if we will bow to the putting on. It is an action process through life that takes off the old and puts on the new. It takes want-to, and it often leads to sufferings. It is through the living of life that fashions and forms us as we walk together in a God-provoked mindset of humility that characterizes true godly servanthood, in my understanding.

In simplicity, I have a daily choice to put on an attitude of humility no matter who I am with, regardless of where I am, or what I am engaged in. Humility is a bowing to this truth; I am not more than, I am not less than, but I am equal to all but God. Equality is not subservience. Equality is not superiority. Equality does not negate humility. Equality is simply an understanding that leads to the great golden rule ... do unto others as you would have them do unto you.

The mini life stories found within this book record a journey of spiritually-discovered humility while walking with others and simultaneously surrendering self into the loving, forming hands of God.

Table of Contents

III. **The Five Senses** *Continued*

IV. **Cross Cultural** 89

Understanding God's ways experientially versus academically is a journey with the Holy Spirit that will humble the proud and set firm foundations.

V. **Classics** 111

Teachings that stand the test of time.

VI. Challenges 137

With breath comes challenge, and through the journey of life to our individual grand finale, challenges will be ever present. Will we embrace challenge?

VII. Nature, Things Great and Small Teach 161

The majesty of creation within nature and the animal kingdom beckons man to come and see, come and find God and self in their midst.

VIII. A Tapestry 181

Bits and Pieces. Little by little and day by day character in formation.

INTRODUCTION

Becoming A Disciple

*And all of you must put on the apron of humility, to serve one another;
for the scripture says, "God resists the proud, but shows favor to the humble."*
1 Peter 5:5 GNT

his "mini" compilation of life stories is dedicated to my grand-mother, Lola B. Lehr Strawn, who continues to be my ideal of a Christian, worthy of emulation. You would not find her in church often. She held no worldly offices or titles. But something called love and un-conditional acceptance radiated from within her toward those in her presence. She was a God calling card of peace in her quiet ways. Like Timothy's grandmother of biblical fame, my grandmother is my known root of spiritual heritage. And from her, my mother's spiritual flame was ignited and then mine. Only God knows fully who has been touched by our lives, anyone's life, and to Him alone belongs any praise. We simply are the clay in whom He decided to give life.

Many years ago in the depths of my being, this was etched: "To write what I see and hear in the spirit, to speak and write for His glory." For some I pray this simple effort of obedience will bring a type of new life, perhaps a new perspective, on certain aspects of thought-life through the selection of these shared stories and the many questions posed. Others may pass by without being touched. For this, I can do nothing but ask God to take those into a pasture that will feed and/or supply them in their needed manner. The adage that one man's treasure is another man's junk may be fitting. This comforts me in some strange way.

I had often felt left behind and not a genuine part of my own genera-tion, nor extremely comfortable in my own culture. I have never had a five- or twenty-five-year plan. I had no inner vision or direction for my future, nor did I even think I would live to be forty. That seemed like an eternity. These patterns of planning were for other people, people who thought in ways that I could not comprehend. I just lived in my day. It is not an approach I would suggest in a cultural system as ours. But then God… A criminal justice professor dubbed me "a generalist in a specialist's world." He got it right. He was prophetic when I did not know anything about the language of the Book, let alone The Book, The Bible.

I will begin with "*The Apron …*" title

I never have been a girlie girl. I would rather have been outdoors watching the clouds go by than indoors doing such essential household practices as cooking and sewing. Not that I cannot boil, bake, steam, and fry, but after growing up in the restaurant business, any genuine inclinations were worked out of me quite early.

Then there is sewing. I was introduced to it while in a home economics class that was not of my choosing. To successfully finish the course, a project had to be completed, and that is at the root of the title, *The Apron of Humility*. My project would be an apron, and the beneficiary would be my grandmother, whom I clearly knew loved me unconditionally. The finished product design is forever etched in my mind's eye. Pastel pieces of pinks and greens, yellows and blues camouflaged the one front pocket and two narrow ties that met in the back. It was as simple as I am.

All else is a blur these many years later, but I can tell you my grandmother received my lowly gift and wore it in my presence, and it spoke volumes of love to me. My teacher, on the other hand, sent a note home stating "sewing is not her forte, but I commend her stick-to-itiveness." She applauded me for my staying power in her mandated assignment, but it was not one of love. It was to me an apron of humiliation; it was an embarrassment, mortification, a shame. I can still see the stitching. It would have failed a field sobriety test. Zigs and zags were evidenced all over the fabric. The sewing machine outpaced my abilities with bobbins, thread, needles, hands, and feet. I was out of my element in coordination and interest.

Life continues, years pass, with an ever-present haunting query: What would be my forte? To this day, I am not sure I have been granted eyes to see unambiguously, but it has been my intent for the past many, many years now to simply trust and obey as I complete what I call my *pea patch assignments*, whether in human service positions or ministerial roles. *The Apron of Humility* is another assignment on "the way."

These writings present portions of my own journey with others in various seasons, which ultimately present a glimpse of "Becoming a Disciple." It is in the simplicity of day to day living that we are made and fashioned into His image. It is in simplicity that I think, speak, and now write. Theological dissertations and hypotheses are for the sphere of another, as are Christian novels and even daily devotionals. Each Mini is a self-contained life lesson that is common to man …

Thus, simply defined, this collection of "Mini writings" is my gallery of moments in life that have spoken to me in various ways by questions asked, truths pronounced, and mysteries displayed that remain as life's dangling participles …

I

RELATIONSHIPS

Natural and Spiritual

I

RELATIONSHIPS

Natural and Spiritual

We all need people. We may not like to, but we need people.
God made it that way. He is relational and therefore we are.
An enriched life is a life full of diverse voices.

These Minis are of flesh and blood and of the spirit family, co-equal because when God declares both as family, literally, who is to disagree. Never was it made more clear than when God spoke to me on a train heading for Philadelphia, Pennsylvania, to go pray for Devon and tell him about Jesus. God said, "Devon, brother," not step-brother. Shortly after, I was in Switzerland with a native from Germany that I met in the States. God said, "Jutta, sister." It happened once again when flying over the ocean and back to the States from Burundi when the Holy Spirit whispered, "Sophone," and simultaneously flashed his face before me stating, "He is your brother."

The wrestle with who is my brother and who is my sister was finally and definitively over. It was finished. The voice of God within penetrated and perforated the natural definition of family. If in Christ, whether red, yellow, black, brown, or white, on this continent or that continent, we are all truly one family.

Last Car to The Gap,
The Call of the Troll Man

For God so loved this son, He gave His Son.

As my dad lay dying, we had some illuminating conversations. It took the knock of death on his personal door to make room for the conversations, but nevertheless, we had them. I cherish those few days but not the circumstances. As he was sharing a variety of events from his very colorful life, one struck me deeply.

He shared that as a young boy, he had the opportunity to hang out with the coal miners after their long, dirty, and tiring shifts because his dad was one of them. My grandfather had a particularly good position, if there was such a thing in that line of work. He oversaw the animal stables, as mules were used then to bring the coal out of the veins, deep inside the earth.

Within this conversation, the statement that caught my attention was the cry of the Troll Man: *"Last car to The Gap. This is the last car to The Gap. Get on board."* For most of the men, the trolley was the one-and-only way home. They literally could not afford to miss the last car back home to The Gap, or they would be left to their own devices …

And now, though my heart was heavy for my dad, it was quickened. A final call to him was approaching, some seventy plus years away from The Gap, which was his boyhood region. He was given eight weeks to live. God was calling, and there was no denying it. This was the last call. Would he board?

I sat beside his bed as a daughter, but in a greater role as a minister, and I watched as reality confronted a very prideful man. As confessions of years of memories were voiced, my dad could finally receive the graces and mercies offered him by a loving God whom he had heard about in his youth. A personal journey from head to heart had reached its zenith … For him, the call of Jesus was now heard as the voice of the Troll Man calling, *"Get on board!"*

Peace, true peace, had finally touched him.

A keystone reminder: Hope abounds while there is life.
Give God your voice. Commit it to Him.
It just may be used like the Voice of The Troll Man.

I Am Not Afraid of Dying, But Can You Tell Me How to Live?

*T*hese words will haunt me for as long as I live, and I have concluded it is good. My sister presented this statement-query to me within the last year of her life. It was the cry of a person drowning from unrelenting physical sufferings. Those conditions were frightening, and she was out of control. Even as her body was failing her, her mind was searching for a way of survival. My sister was fighting a losing battle with chronic pain, an undiagnosed heart condition, varieties of drugs and alcohol, as well as being disheartened from years of strained and terminated relations. She could not cope. This fiercely independent, highly intelligent, vibrant character could not ...

Like so many others in Christendom, it was not the issue of her end time destination that was unsettling, but life itself. She seemed able to entrust her death to a capable God, but in actual day to day living, her trying seemed to be in vain. She could not fully release herself into the hands of God. When in the throes of severe bouts with physical and mental exhaustion, which were frequent visitors to her temple, she would indeed reach out for spiritual comfort and peace in her local house of worship occasionally or via phone conversations with me routinely. Often those calls and her cries came in the wee hours of the morning when her pain would not succumb to the medical remedies prescribed nor her self-prescribed street methods of pain relief. However, and invariably, at the scent of any sign of temporary relief, she would be up and running, ordering life again on her own terms. Sound familiar?

Can you tell me how to live was her genuine mantra, but what in the end left her lonely, isolated, angry, and scrambling for true comfort was her inability to apprehend the Word of God as a viable, contemporary road map to her quest for inner peace. Thinking there had to be more than words written in a book of old to guide her, she mistakenly overlooked the very lifeboat designed just for her query, "How am I intended to live?" The very medicine she cried out for, she rejected. I say it again. She rejected the way to true peace amid her trials because she could not embrace the tenet of God as Lord … here and now.

That is what Life in the Spirit is all about: *His Lordship here and now.*

Lordship

How shall we live but by the Word of God? We must grasp this simple truth. The one gift we can give to anyone that will never return void is The Word. Therefore, let us be free within ourselves to share. Let us remember that at some point in time, someone had the courage to share this lifeline with us.

I miss my sister. Not too long ago, I was listening to the radio when I heard one of her favorite songs, *What A Wonderful World*. I could not help thinking how truly wonderful it is for her now.

Life and death are not in our hands.
The ability to listen and love are.

Black-eyed Susans,
A Family Portrait

One day, while walking at a leisurely pace, I saw something that stirred me deeply. I had been walking the same road every spring, summer, autumn, and winter for a few years, but this day, I want to repeat that I saw something I had not seen before. What I clearly saw was a family of Black-eyed Susans. These flowers were grouped together in such a way that it was as though they deliberately were gathered and posing for a family portrait. From a distance, they glistened, glowed, blended, and complimented one another. It was a wonderful sight to observe.

But as I approached the bank they were gathered on, the stand of flowers began to take on their own unique, individual appearances. Close up and personal, some of these flowers looked anything but appealing. Some looked as though a dog had chewed on their ears. The petals were tattered and torn. The coloring of some had been faded and washed out, and their stems were brown and limp, not green and hardy. Still others were bent over, unable to hold their heads up, as though from the weight of their lives. Only a few seemed slightly flawed and even fewer appeared gorgeous, vibrant, and erect.

If these flowers were people, we would say the majority were rather plain, broken, and unattractive in appearance. We would not prize them or parade them before those we esteem. Rather, we would tuck them away from the scrutiny of others, ashamed and embarrassed by the very thought of their humanity and even more so of the family connection.

I saw a family portrait of Black-eyed Susans that day, but in reality, I witnessed the family of God in all her beauty from a distance and all her imperfections upon closer scrutiny. In that moment of time, I experienced our Heavenly Father's love afresh for His body of imperfect children, individually and collectively. He is not ashamed of us, as we so often are of ourselves and others. Our imperfections and brokenness are His opportunities to make and mold us as we walk with Him, here on earth, where we have been planted for a season.

Ponder this. We are family. The body of Christ is like the portrait of the Black-eyed Susans positioned to be seen in all their frailty, humility, and glory.

Amanda's Lesson

One of my nieces graduated with honors from high school. In fact, she was the valedictorian of her class. Traditionally, the role of valedictorian would include giving a farewell speech to the graduating class, mixed with quips about the past and hope for the future. Amanda, however, opted out of this portion of her honor. When my sister asked why she did not want to speak, she simply said she did not have anything to say.

In the natural, we would think this is just the type of person to have something to say. Her academic and civic involvements declared her a young achiever, a leader with proven abilities.

At first, I found this puzzling and thought she missed a wonderful opportunity. On further reflection, I concluded that perhaps she did say what she had to say already, by her choices and actions that were evidenced in her school record. She spoke, but it was in a non-public voice.

How often have we clamored toward the one who says by their actions "see me-hear me" and missed the beauty of those who operate by choice of disposition in a more reserved expression or manner? How many persons have we passed by who walked quietly? How many times would an action on our part, with less verbiage, have been more, in various situations?

I have gleaned from Amanda's decision. Her voice did resonate most loudly the night of her graduation by giving room for someone else's voice to be recognized.

In appropriate situations, would we be willing
to model the same maturity?

On Running The Race

Hebrews 12

*A*s autumn wrapped itself up by the shedding of color as well as leaves and began making room for a new season, my mind wandered to cycles, the passing of torches, and the running of races.

This period had been bursting with lessons and meditations concerning running a race. It brought to remembrance a conversation I had several years ago with a young man full of enthusiasm and brimming with questions concerning matters of God. Among various issues, he wanted to know about my prayer life. I carefully considered the question, then responded knowing my reply would not be typical to the times.

Presently, we are living in an age of formulas. The things of God and of His Church have not escaped the milieu. Everything seems to have a recipe. Run, walk, swim, hike ... put your body in motion at least every other day for health. Eat a variety of colorful fruits and vegetables, minus red meat, but include fish for optimum well-being. Add calcium, a good multi-vitamin, and sleep at least seven hours. Drink a glass of wine for health, and tell three young people weekly what a good job they are doing. Good job. Good job. Good job. The exact phraseology is a must. Anything less would demean and deflate. And so goes the very uniform, linear type Western methodology presented for most everything under the sun concerning the issues of life.

The question my young friend posed needed a spirit response. It would have been extremely easy to recite what I did or did not do in my prayer time, but I answered his query with a query. What is God asking of you? Is it five minutes, sixty minutes, or eight hours a day? Is it in the morning, at noon, or the midnight hour? Are you to pray indoors, outdoors, sitting, standing, or lying prostrate before Him? Does it matter? Will it always be the same? You must learn to hear the voice of God for yourself. Ask, seek, knock for God's desire for you in prayer. He will meet and instruct you as you go before Him. Trust.

Christianity at its root was never intended to be an uninspired variety of spirituality or religion, although many leaders have modeled, taught, and insisted it is: "*It*" being "*their*" way, not necessarily directed by the Holy Spirit. These leaders mandate *reading through the Bible three times a year, committing to memory at least five verses a month, and worshipping by an exact combination of three upbeat praise songs followed by three hymns. No deviation allowed. Church cannot be missed for the sake of growth, no exceptions. Attendance not permitted elsewhere for the sake of unity. Grow where planted. Plant where instructed. Forget harvesting. You are not qualified.*

Now is the time to mature. When we are free, we can proclaim freedom to others. Jesus is the Author and Perfecter of … our own faith. We are to be running very personal races that have been set before us individually by a very personal God. We must hear for ourselves. We must teach this truth. Pass the torch. To share an idea or principle is valid. To order it is dogmatic and oppressive and leaves little room for a flowing prayer life in the spirit.

Whose race are we running anyway? To be authentic, it must be *my* own. It must be *your* own.

Sacred is the journey
to discovery and rediscovery of spiritual disciplines
as we find our authentic way through life with God.

The Wood Pile and The Ten Virgins

*W*inter was still in progress in upstate New York when my older sister and I were engaged in one of our normal weekly chats about this and that and nothing. I have always wondered what our conversations would seem like to anyone listening in: perhaps like code. But really, it does not matter what anyone would think as it is our way of loving one another from a distance on Sunday afternoons.

What is of importance has to do with her wood pile, or lack thereof, near the end of a passing harsh winter season. I was absolutely flabbergasted to hear that she had nearly run out of wood before winter had wrapped itself up. If she were a neophyte to the North Country perhaps, I could have understood the under-planning. However, this is far from the truth. My sister is a veteran of the realities of the gray, cold, snowy, conditions of winter that extend for most of five months in the Adirondacks. She should not have been caught off guard, yet was.

We are instructed through the parable of the Ten Virgins that we must be fully awake and prepared for His Harvest of our life … for it can come at any time. We read that five virgins were prepared because their spiritual houses were in order, and five were not. Those who did not have their oil for the due season were shut out: no exceptions and no secondary excuses were entertained.

I ask, is your woodpile stocked or your oil lamp full as a veteran of the things of God?

I propose, if you are not yet a believer in the God of Christianity, today is the day to say yes to the great love of Jesus Christ, for He is the only acceptable Fuel Source that can bring you safely into the Kingdom of God for all of eternity. He awaits your yes.

Consider this. We all have a common charge, whether we are novices or experienced in the things of God. *We cannot afford to be found dozing, as my sister had been with her wood pile that year. Our destinies and the destinies of others may be at stake.*

Joseph's Pit, Sibling Rivalry

Genesis 37

*A*s Jesus gathered in the Upper Room with His followers at the Last Supper, we hear, "Do this in remembrance of Me." This command is an ordinance of the church that is implemented around the world wherever and whenever Christians meet. The elements of bread, or wafer, wine, or juice, are the *symbols chosen to celebrate and remember the life, death, and resurrection life of Jesus Christ*, at once, both Man and God fully divine. It is a holy commemoration and a time for reflection, attitude correction, forgiveness, and divine healing. *Celebrated* restoration between man and God is the absolute result for the person who consciously partakes of the Lord's Supper, or communion, as it is also known. It is a remembrance of the cost of our restoration. Jesus Himself instituted this regulation, but not for the purpose of division or separation. Rather, it was for the depiction of unity. It is a designated meeting place with Him for all of God's children. No one who has accepted the Son of God, Jesus Christ, is to be barred from His Table.

Regardless of man's meddling, it is holy, and God is waiting to meet us there any time. This truth is liberating. Communion is a covenantal remembrance and a dependence on Christ, as well as a community gathering place, for all in the kingdom.

Sibling rivalry has always been a part of our human condition, and before it was manifested in the Garden of Eden, we see it evidenced in heavenly places. Satan himself, although not a sibling of God, envied God, and that spirit of jealousy has been at the core of war ever since. Satan continues to envy and do battles with God and His people; angels of light continue to fight angels of darkness, and brothers and sisters and nations continue to brawl with one another in the natural and spiritual realms. Succinctly, at the root lies jealousy. There is, as we read in Ecclesiastes, nothing new under the sun.

Query: Who have you ever deemed as troublesome competition or marked as dead weight and quite dispensable? How deeply has rivalry touched your life? Have you ever singlehandedly, or in harmony with community, decided someone had to be banished because of an arbitrary rule instituted for the furtherance of your/our own kingdom to come?

Restoration

At the Table of Communion is where forgiveness and reconciliation await us. It is there that we acknowledge our sin of jealousy and our rivalries within and without the House of God. For it is there, at His Table, where we ask God to restore our relationships that we have recklessly, deliberately, and sometimes even unintentionally discarded. May our rivals of any size, shape, race, creed, tongue, gender, and so on, whom we have thrown to the wind forgive us as well.

May this be our new day.

No to Rivalry wherever it is found.

What Would You Do?

I had a brief conversation with my sister that I have not been able to set aside. She shared with me an encounter her son had at a gas station he randomly stopped at on his return home from visiting with a friend out of state.

It was about four-thirty in the morning when he pulled up to the gas pump, got out of his old car, and started the process of activating the purchase with his credit card. A middle-aged man on the other side of the pump, driving an old Bronco, asked him quietly if he would put six gallons of gasoline in his car, stating that he did not have any money and was on his way to work. In return, my six-foot, two hundred-pound, well-educated, and very-articulate nephew, without engaging in any more conversation, simply stretched the hose to the other side, pumped out exactly six gallons of gasoline into the stranger's vehicle, and then proceeded to fill his own car before continuing down the highway, many miles yet to go before reaching his home.

Later, he called his mom and asked the question, "What would you have done?"

My sister then called me and asked what I would have done.

I feel compelled to ask God what can be gleaned from the field of this strikingly odd occurrence in the early morning hours when most of Montana and the country would be either already at work or at home in bed. The timing seemed suspicious.

Many may ask what there is to consider: there was a person in need and a person to meet the need; therefore, case closed. Yet, I must wonder if there is not more to be gleaned from this incident. Was the gasoline encounter just a random meeting of two travelers brought on by one party's straightforward forgetfulness because he left wallet and money at home? Was the lack of verbal conversation a necessary part of the scenario to be played out? Was my nephew's willingness to help or not to help a stranger in need part of the picture in play? Did visual clues of the old, battered

Bronco speak volumes that the man's needs could be legitimate? Was the early childhood training my nephew received of doing unto others as you would like done unto you, automatically the cause of his response to pump and pay? Did the age differential play a role and release empathy within him that whispered, that could be me one day?

All that transpired will never really be known, nor why the encounter happened in the first place. What I do know is that I do not truly know what I would have done in the wee hours of that morning. One element within says yes, I would have done the same as my nephew, with no questions asked. Another fraction of me says no, the stranger's story is suspect. And then I seem checked within and think what about our economic times. Is this a precursor or likely picture that will be played out more and more around our nation? Will we be asked to pump and pay on behalf of the genuinely working poor and disenfranchised? As a reminder, it is written, God said some will entertain Angels without knowing. Only He knows … (Hebrews 13:2).

What would you have done?
Discerning is imperative. It is in the small things that we learn to hear.
We must continually ask God to grant us the wisdom to know
what to do when and with whom?
It is, in fact, a discipline for life.

Who But God?

John 15   Psalm 139

*T*here is an old Negro spiritual that goes something like this:

> Nobody knows the trouble I've seen
> Nobody knows my sorrow
> Nobody knows the trouble I've seen
> Glory, Hallelujah.

The Church

God's gracious love and provision is generally known within the church. But this is about just one. Yes, about one of His lost sheep.

Outside the sheep gate stood a lonely and shattered individual. Separated from loved ones and isolated by other behavioral circumstances, this person was slowly and deliberately befriended by another, a Christian. Over a course of months, one caring human being multiplied into many, and a circle of love was soon encompassing the once solitary being. Prayers were being offered from near and far on her behalf. Shelter, counsel, friendship, and money was heaped upon the lost one and manifested change was evident. The old was passing away, and new life was springing forth in thought and demeanor.

However, an all too familiar unraveling that began in secret became manifest. Slowly, counsel became less important, and steps of accountability were skirted. Christian relationships were being exchanged, and the continued offer of God's spiritual wine was passed by for the old, comfortable, inexpensive man-made bottled wine found on a store shelf. Almost audibly, the patterned thinking of old began to play all through the one recently found, but seemingly lost again. Nobody knows the trouble I am in, and nobody seems to care, but alcohol. Yes, alcohol knows my sorrows.

What transpired? To the natural eye, it appeared the undertaking and heaping upon of genuine love was a loss. The exchange of the new for the old once again seemed to express failure and impotency on the part of God and His people. At nearly the same time, in the form of a question illumination came to the fore: Who or what is the genuine inspector of fruit, fruitfulness, and genuineness? As it was in the past, it continues to be, and will forever be, God's ultimate domain. We must leave the outcome to his infinite knowing. For who but God truly knows all things?

At the beginning and ending of every day, we must commit to God our human assignments for His safe keeping. If you are discouraged, take heart. Every directed obedience and gift given in His name will not return to the Master void. What looks like loss and lost forever to us is not with Him? Keep answering His call to go and be and do for His lost sheep, as we are the *triumphant Church*, despite how things seem. Be encouraged.

Who but God knows the sorrow of a heart?

Who but God knows how to make it whole?

Holes in Souls, Go Tell

Acts 1   Mark 6

*Y*ears ago, just prior to my return to the States after ministering in Europe, God said to me to "… go to your sisters and tell them, *God wants to heal the holes in your souls*, even as I am healing yours. I want you to buy Swiss cheese to use as an example of the holes, and then I want you to take communion together." There were no further instructions.

My relationship with my sisters to this point was not on a spiritual plain. We were blood sisters but not God sisters. I lived my life, and they lived theirs, as we kept in touch with one another by phone across the miles. Inwardly, I wondered how this would come to pass as one sister lived in New York, the other in California, and I was in North Carolina. Nevertheless, within a short period of time, the three of us were sitting together in California talking about our lives and God's desire to bring us into a place of deeper healing. I bought the cheese, and we took communion together as instructed. It was the first time for communion, and unknown to us then, it would be the final time we would be together before one sister's unexpected death a few years later. But it opened a new doorway for us to walk through together that included the God of our mother.

As unsettling and uncomfortable as it was in the beginning to introduce a spiritual component with my sisters for a myriad of natural reasons, it became a gift to me. As the youngest of the three girls, it finally seemed I had something of worth to share with my sisters, whom I always considered more accomplished in all things.

A short time later, when I was on a train traveling from New York to Maryland to visit my biological father and his family, God interrupted my inner musings with a spirit impression: *Go tell your brother about Me.* God said brother, not stepbrother. *Next round of a spiritual encounter,* I thought uncomfortably. But it too came to pass. I shared God was knocking, God loved him, and he ultimately had a personal decision to make. It was clean and simple.

To this day, I still do not know if he decided to embrace Christ, but I entrust Devon to the One who sent me to go tell. This much I know, he is equally loved … God does not have stepchildren. He only has children. He calls them sons and daughters.

To Go Tell those whom we are closest to, those who know us in the natural, is a more weighty matter than those we have no intimacy with. Jesus stated that a prophet is not honored in their native territory. Yet, to be enabled in one's Jerusalem … is to be strengthened at one's core. Courage follows, and it is preparatory for Samaria and finally for the outer parts of the world.

At the end of the day, God is always found faithful,
for where He guides, it is said He provides.
We are met in our obedience.
Trust in and through the uncomfortable.

Multiplication

Matthew 14

*I*t was a time of get-together. Family and friends, old and new, gathered around a table that was often extended to its maximum capacity to accommodate those from varied places and conventions. Conversation was diverse and flowed freely in different rooms as the final preparations and setting of the table was completed. On cue, everyone merged to the table finding their place of invitation. Thanksgiving was offered, and then the bird was unveiled.

Instantly, it seemed everyone knew the improbable mathematics concerning the size of the free-range chicken and the number of people who were to partake of it, although not a word was murmured. One by one and with pleasantness, each guest took a sliver of the bird, a shard, a minuscule portion, as though it was not the center piece of the main course. Or was it imagination? No, politeness and etiquette ruled amongst the robust statured guests. Miss Manners, the recognized sage of all things refined and of social propriety in the nation would have been delighted and readily set her seal of approval upon each elder and younger person present.

Yet, the still small voice of God stirred within. Quietly, almost imperceptibly, as deer are known to enter a scene, the word multiplication came, followed by the biblical narrative of the fishes and loaves of bread. As the thoughts whirled within and the genial banter without, I was made full, yet not of bird.

Time passed swiftly, and as the gathering ended with the slow migrating of individuals away from the table, the schooling of The Spirit was just beginning to unfold.

Multiplication and the Need of Circumstances

It is written in scripture that on several occasions when the gathering of thousands of hungry souls came before the Man from Galilee, and the natural food supply was limited to a handful of fish and a few paltry loaves of bread, the circumstances created a perfect storm in terms of hospitality and well-being. Yet, He, with simple thanksgiving to His Father, supplied an overabundance of sustaining provision. Further, when a widow woman was left with bare cupboards and only enough provision for her and her son's last supper, a man of God named Elijah, who himself had nothing in the natural, but had faith in the spirit, presented the widow with an alternative option. Give me the first of your meal, and then you will see what can be done. In giving first of what she did have, all her household needs were met. Additionally recorded, we are told there was another woman whose husband had died and left her with two sons and enormous debt. Following tradition, the widow's sons were about to be sold, enslaved to satisfy the families monetary obligations, another man of God known as Elisha intervened. He asked the widow woman what was in her house. In response, she offered to the prophet a jar full of oil and multiple empty vessels borrowed from neighbors. Once again, a simple act of obedience was used to meet their dire condition of need.

Believing

What circumstance may be before you today that requires a multiplication factor? Limitations were unwittingly placed by etiquette that Thanksgiving day. No one mentioned the obvious inadequacy of the chicken's size to feed all the people present. Therefore, even the possibility to eye witness the miracle of multiplication was impeded. No one asked for more.

Questions remain. Was the arm and power of God bound by a simple act of not asking? Will we believe provision waits for the individual or corporate presentation of need? Will we believe the exercise of faith is involved in the manifestation of the needed provision? God says He is the same yesterday, today, and forever …

Do we believe? Do we honestly, unequivocally believe
He desires to provide all good things …

Friendship

*G*eorge Eliot wrote in "The Essence of Friendship": *Oh, the comfort, the inexpressible comfort of feeling safe with a person; having neither to weigh thoughts nor measure words, but to pour them all out, just as they are, chaff and grain together, knowing that a faithful hand will take and sift them, keep what is worth keeping, and then, with the breath of kindness, blow the rest away.* Eliot, through this poem, masterfully defines in a few words the best in earthly friendships and the finest relational work of the church, and most notably and poignantly expresses without personal knowledge of the free-flowing intimacy between God and His children experienced via prayer.

It is in prayer that our intents and desires are made known to God. Eliot says a knowing hand differentiates between that which is worthy and that which is not. And as a child of God, it is in His answers, and at times ostensible lack of them, that we experience His omniscient, omnipotent love. In fact, the breath of kindness that blows away chaff *fulfills the divine law of love* ... it covers a brother's darkness, it covers our own darkness.

A Proposal:
It would be well with our souls if we *practiced* this poem.
It would be well with our souls if we *became* this poem.
It is good to have a trusted friend. It is a *gift* to be a *trusted friend.*
It is best to know Jesus, as Friend, who will never leave nor forsake.

May we become and be known as safe havens ...

Note: The writer George Elliot was a *woman* and a confirmed Atheist. She, *yes, she,* did not envision or partake of Jesus as Friend, according to public records.

II

FIRST THE NATURAL,
THEN THE SPIRITUAL

II

FIRST THE NATURAL,
THEN THE SPIRITUAL

1 Corinthians 15

God says look intensely at those things around you.
Walk closely with Me, and you will perceive My spirit realm.

*P*racticed daily, it becomes a continual adventure with the Holy Spirit that will expand, intrigue, and delight your soul and spirit.

French Fries and
Other Related Matter

*F*or a short season, I had an unusual and unexplainable desire come over me, seemingly out of nowhere, for French fries. It was on the heels of an experience involving two different books with different subject matter suggested by two different people from two different coasts as "must reads" by Christian writers of our day. Upon opening, these new books literally reeked of regurgitation. It was unsettling!

With the onset of the French fry attack, I started on a journey to satisfy the overwhelming desire for them, and this unexplainable natural hunger led me over the next few weeks to order after order of cold, limp, soggy fries that were saturated with oil and were as repulsive in color as taste. The experience was uncanny. It was inconceivable that a person could go to multiple type restaurants, as well as locales, over a short period of time and experience this phenomena.

Following the fries incident, I visited a familiar church led by a pastor I had known for years. Soon after the conversation with the pastor, I received a call from a person I have known personally and professionally for many years. As we engaged freely in banter, as we often did, an odd sense of "old" washed over me, and then a knowing. Light was finally replacing the dimness in my understanding concerning these different but similar scenarios. Simply put, the books that oozed of foulness, the French fries that were rancid, the church pastor, and my relationship with an old friend all had a commonality. The word that I heard in my spirit was "old." As I pondered the word, I sought for greater clarity. The foul and old that manifested through the books, the French fries, the church pastor, and friend all pointed to a deficiency of life, and all needed rejuvenation, flavor, truth, and verdancy.

The query is what or who may be touching your life that reeks of acridity, vomitus, and flatness? What has the feel of limpness, parchedness, and a discolored appearance? Has complacency and self-righteousness brought a drought in teachability, flexibility, ingenuity, and usability?

God desires more. In the wilderness, He provided *fresh* manna for the Israelites. Numbers records that the people gathered and made cakes, which were baked with *fresh* oil and tasted accordingly unlike my French fries. In Psalms and Job and a myriad of other places in The Word, it says that His glory and anointing are *fresh* and generously poured out for those willing to receive in their due season. We learn that His Spirit gives strength, vitality, and creative unction when sought after. The aroma of continual presence is as sweet as the Rose of Sharon.

Determine to and prepare for the scrutiny of the Spirit of God to make assessment in conjunction with you, as to what needs re*fresh*ing, revitalizing, repruning in your life, not the life of any other. God's life-giving Spirit is anything but colorless, parched, acrid, or sterile. If His people are experiencing these things routinely, there is a certainty of a disconnection from their Source.

Choose life. Abandon or banish lifelessness, dullness in all its forms, from relationships, to programs, plans, approaches, methods, and teachings held too tightly. Put everything on the table for review, self-satisfaction as well. Finally, let God be God, and He will blow afresh.

There is nothing tasty or becoming about old oil. There is nothing becoming about old, outdated modes. Nothing.

Life in the Spirit is about change and exchange.
To be a living sacrifice is to bring an end to, conclude, terminate,
die to, expire to, SELF. New life awaits.

Capacities

What about Capacities?

*A*ll elements of life on earth are limited. Space, not outer space, has boundaries or capacities. There is only so much space on discs. Computers and phone chips hold a limited amount of memory. Drawers, walls, and floor space in our dwellings are limited by area. Planes, trains, buses, and ships have passenger or cargo limitations. Our oceans have only so much depth, and our mountains so much peak. Humans are truncated by our abilities—capacities in memory, eating, drinking, reading, running, creating, traveling, sleeping, and on and on. We are capped, as is our present knowledge of the earth and its elements. We are not as fluid as our mathematical calculations of ad infinitum, at least yet. In short, our mortal state keeps us in check.

Walking Pack Rats

Why is it that so many of us continually buy and stuff and stuff and buy into our finite spaces? When our surroundings are intolerably full, we simply expand into borrowed or rented storage space. The concept of maxed or limited capacity is in fact an abomination to many, if you have eyes to see. There is an abundance of unwillingness to accept established boundaries. Perhaps it is time to take inventory. We must look in the mirror of self, both natural and spirit, and address a remarkably simple question. Am I a walking pack rat carrying on or in me excessive baggage of any sort? And if so, how is it impacting my world and those around me?

Jesus addressed a similar issue of goods and capacities in this way found in a parable in Luke 5:37-39 (NIV), "*And no one pours new wine into old wineskins. Otherwise, the new wine will burst the skins; the wine will run out and the wineskins will be ruined. No, new wine must be poured into new wineskins. And no one after drinking old wine wants the new, for they say, 'The old is better.'* "

Can you hear the call to and necessity for change if our tomorrows are to be dissimilar? This parable clearly speaks of the capacities of containers, the usefulness of that which is contained as well as the consequences of fusion or interchange between that which is old and new. Some elements must leave in order to make room for new.

Position yourself in the coming days to hear afresh from God. What needs to fade away in your life to facilitate the new? What excesses may you be carrying in your thought processes, patterns of behavior or doctrines? Are your capacities in accord with that which is being consumed in both the natural and spirit realms? Is there an overflow of old coming from your life that is contaminating the budding new? Finally, does God want to enlarge you, but you have deeply rooted yourself in days gone by and are content to stay the same? Are you fearful of change?

Capacities, abilities, and boundaries touch us all.
Let God have His will and way fully.
Give Him permission to take out and put in as He so wills.
Overflow then will not be a problem,
either in the natural or the spirit realms.

What Was That?

*N*o kidding. We were driving around Palmdale, California, some time ago, and the couple we were with said, "Look over there. What do you see?" As we buzzed by, I glimpsed what seemed to be a tall but scrawny tree. At the second look over my shoulder, I saw a shiny substance through what appeared to be the branches. Although not a botanist, I know that no natural tree bark has glistening properties like something metallic when the sun hits it. And then in an instant we were past the scene altogether. As we dialogued about what we thought we saw, a tall but scrawny tree, perhaps something native to the western states, our hosts broke into hearty laughter. The answer to the mystery tree was soon to be revealed.

Digression

A few months prior to this California trip, I was meditating on an issue and had the thought or impression, *things are not what they seem.* In an instant and after the laughter had subsided, we now knew the tree was not what it seemed to be. Intentionally positioned within a cluster of native trees to California, this tree in question was finally identified as the imposter it was. What appeared to be a tree as we zoomed by at seventy-five miles per hour was, in fact, identified by our hosts as a cell tower dressed like a tree. *Yes, a cell tower dressed as a tree.*

Things are not always what they seem, nor are people always what they seem. This is an uncomfortable truth that becomes even more uncomfortable when we are addressing the issues of the church and her citizens. How, as people of God, individually and collectively, are we perceived when people cruise by our lives, whether at five or seventy-five miles per hour?

No one should ever have to look back and wonder …
what was that, what was that.

Seeing This Ol' House

*W*e were walking down a corridor, two of us quietly commenting on the shoddy, disrepair of the building when a pleasant male voice piped in from behind and said: "We did all this work ourselves. We even have an upstairs." He spoke with a great deal of love and affection for what he was seeing in this ol' house of worship, that belied our sight. The incongruence was astounding. A giant gulf existed between perceptions. Someone was not seeing. Who matters, but the why, seems to loom as the greater mystery. Why, is the question that plays havoc within? What caused the dimness of eye and perception of beauty when it was so enormously contrary to a natural accuracy of truth? Was it due to personal investment only because they were his hands that painstakingly and lovingly built and rebuilt, painted, scraped, and cleaned something that was in far greater disrepair than the present-day appearance? Or perhaps, within his mind's eye, he holds a picture of its former condition not unlike a young bride and groom who sixty years later envision one another as though it was their wedding night. The wrinkled skin, added weight, thinning hair, and slowed gait are as though they are not. Is the dimming of the eye and the comfortableness of an old shoe a gift?

To the lovers of old there seems no harm. They are seeing and feeling with their hearts, and it rightly seems a gift. Yet, for the ol' house, it holds a differing weight in both natural and spiritual contexts. The consequences of its reality could be perilous.

Does seeing really matter? To the lovers of old, we say no. To those still on their journey to always seek and find truth, we must say yes. This house of worship needs repair as does the mind-spirit of the worshiper. For to see things as they were and not as they are is to live in a place of danger. Exaggeration? Hear the cry of the Spirit of God.

From the beginning of recorded biblical time, God has asked, pleaded, and sent to His people, voices of men, women, and even of beasts, such as

Balaam's ass to say, *Open your eyes. See as I see.* And yet it seems that only a remnant will respond in each generation. Are you one?

We must desire to see, to discern things as they are,
for times like these are wrapped in variations of deception
and in hues that are not voluntarily transparent.

Esse Quam Videri
"To Be What You Seem"
Joan of Ark

$\mathcal{T}$he nations are full of counterfeit products. From sea to shining sea these goods, whether they are tomatoes or potatoes, chickens or corn, are flooding the markets. Women's handbags, men's watches, dresses, suits, and even inauthentic cars are being found in king's palaces and the poor palaces alike. The disenfranchised have them because they cannot afford the genuine, and the rich have them to imitate the richer, and the richest have them for insurance purposes. Indeed, the world is infested with the imposters of goods.

One Day ...

One day, a young man sat outside the door of the church I attended begging for spare change. He was attired in torn dirty jeans and was shoeless. The odor that emanated from him was as strong as his young body looked. He was a sight to behold, but no more so than the many others that can be found sitting in parks or panhandling along the exits of our many highways and by-ways daily.

As people passed, some responded to his request for money and others simply walked by. When church was commencing, he was invited in and reluctantly took a seat at the back of the house to the right of me. I sat quietly and observed as someone brought him a blanket. Another gave him water and yet another brought him a praise book. Others, who never greeted anyone after months of attending, deliberately and purposely welcomed him during the greeting segment of the service. The church was as busy as bees trying to attend to this young man and his seeming needs. And *seeming* is right.

Aaron was a homeless-looking and smelling imposter. He was a plant by the young associate pastor to see if he would be cared for according to the edicts of Christ to feed the hungry, clothe the naked, and visit those imprisoned. Unquestionably, the tenets were followed in the hearts of most that day.

A Few Hours Later …

Later, like a bolt of lightning, I was reminded of a portion of the old story of Joan of Arc who was given a God assignment to go to the King. As she entered the palace of the King, she was surrounded by scores of people who separated her from his throne. He could readily be seen but not as easily approached. With little time to waste, those with her thought the situation was hopeless for Joan to get to the King. But suddenly, after praying and scanning the people slowly, and then "hearing her voices," a phrase we would not use today, she went over to a simply dressed man in the crowd, bowed before him, and said: "Your Highness the King." And yes, it was the true King.

Not unlike the young pastor's attempt at trickery, the King chose a decoy or imposter, to sit on his throne dressed in kingly attire and being attended to as though he was the King to test the authenticity of Joan's giftings. And God showed Himself to be faithful. By His Spirit, He responded to Joan's petition, guiding her to find the King. She did not rely on her natural sight, inclinations, or thoughts. Joan did not ask assistance of any human, or take nor bring any good gift, or extend herself in any way to the counterfeit king sitting on the throne. She bowed only before the true Royal. She was not deceived by what was presented before her natural senses as many in the church were duped that Sunday.

In the days ahead, with the ever-increasing flooding of the counterfeit, the imposters and the inauthentic; the people of God must be adorned in spiritual discernment. It is not enough to follow one's senses only when in the employ of a mighty God. It is not enough to just do 'good things' without asking the Holy Spirit if this is His intention for the hour and circumstances that are before us. It is no longer acceptable to do business as usual and rely on programs and methods of yesterday, no matter how well they worked then. It is not any more acceptable to automatically replicate what the church next door, across the country, or across the ocean is doing today either.

The God of Christianity is an intentional God and a God that has ways and means that we know not of, and will know not of, if we do not seek Him in every and all matters large and small.

Scripture tells us that Jesus did what He saw the Father doing. He said what the Father said and went where the Father sent Him. This was His root of success and will be ours individually and collectively as the body of Christ if we will embrace it as lifestyle.

Christ's model is worthy of following. His agenda is pure. Doing kind, humanitarian acts is good. Doing kind, humanitarian acts in Jesus' name is even better. Doing kind, humanitarian acts in Jesus' name because you discern by the Spirit a genuine, authentic need is best!

Are you what you seem? It is an important question.

It warrants a truthful response.

Esse Quam Videri, To Be What You Seem

The Cupboards of Sister Rita

*M*any years ago, I found myself sitting on a park bench, alone, midday, as a gentle rain fell upon me and my single small suitcase. It had been decided there was no room in my family inn any longer, after my unreserved acceptance of Jesus Christ and subsequent baptism in the Holy Spirit. I was simply no longer the same, and it was disconcerting to those who knew God but not in the same intensity. My giving away the few worldly goods I had made no earthly sense to them. Therefore, because of this momentary family dismissal, I was forced to trust my new God in extremely uncomfortable and previously unknown type situations from the very beginning.

Had I consciously known the seemingly bleak and lonely path right before me I know not if I would have bowed my knee, but then God knows our frailties and works with us accordingly.

Nevertheless, an old friend in a neighboring town, who had little herself, hearing about my newfound situation, invited me to stay for a short period of time. How short the time frame would be came as an unsuspected surprise to both of us when one day her landlord called and stated that the rules in this housing community allowed for visitors for two weeks only. There were no exceptions to the rule, and if found in non-compliance, her lease would be automatically terminated. Being a single mom of two, there was no option but to adhere to policy, and at the end of the two weeks, with a heavy heart, she dropped me off at the local park with neither of us knowing what would happen.

The rain mirrored my inner condition that day. As minutes morphed into hours and dusk was approaching, my inner struggles intensified. All day, I sat hoping, wondering, and praying that my newly found God would make known to me what I was supposed to do, but doubts began to taunt me. *See what accepting Jesus got you. A park bench, no less, in the rain, with no one and no resources to call your own. And you want to follow Him …*

Finally, a flash of a face came before me and an inner sense to call her. Sister Rita was once a Carmelite nun whom I had seen previously at a few Christian gatherings in the region, but I did not know her personally. Nevertheless, I found a phone booth and managed to briefly share my predicament and then was astounded to find she had literally just returned within minutes of my call from a trip out of town. Darkness was closing in, but the night was now turning light. Sister Rita's door opened for exactly six weeks. Peace prevailed. By then, I trusted God enough to believe if one door closes another will open precisely at the point of need. And it did! My life continues to evidence this truth so many years later.

Sister Rita was a lasting influence in my life. I will forever retain the image of her cupboards when residing at Resurrection House. God's provision was astonishing. Her cupboards could not contain the abundant blessings, and this image continues to surface whenever I find myself in doubt. God kept her spiritual and natural cupboards full to overflowing throughout her long life of service. What He has done for her, He can do for me, and for you.

Let us Keep Trusting The One Who is Able
as Our Circumstances Twirl.

Holy, Holy, Holy,
and A Confession of Doubt

*T*he song, *"He's Got the Whole World in His Hands"* is going around and round through me. Is it true? I want it to be true. I want it to be true every day. Jesus Christ, Son of God, Son of Man is said to have the whole world in His hands. Nevertheless, young and old alike are picking up newspapers or tuning into nightly newscasts and unrelentingly being assaulted with horrific sights of inhumanity. It is as though an increasing barrage of hate has been loosed across nations, and it seems unending. How much of war and famine can humanity absorb before we no longer feel, see clearly, or know absolutely?

The biblical record tells us the God of the Christian faith is the God of all love and all power. He spoke, and the sun and moon and stars were placed. Continents were formed, and people groups birthed. Justice. Laws. Mercy. All of life ordered by a wisdom and knowledge higher than man's. Yet, and if all of this is true concerning Jesus, why doesn't it feel like the whole world is safe in His hands today?

As a believer, as a minister, I am not always able to stand tall inwardly or outwardly, when nations bomb nations and poverty and deprivations of every sort abound when I am relatively full, safe, and secure. *Sacrilege,* you may think. *The questioning of your Lord's sovereignty is appalling,* you may say. To this, I whisper haltingly, *I am but dust.* We are frail, doubting, and unbelieving people in the natural. We conclude our queries with answers before we allow the Holy Spirit of truth to penetrate our senses. Feelings and senses are key. No, it does not feel to me some days that the whole world is in Jesus' hands. But when this happens, I acknowledge the very human "wrestle with the doubting Thomas syndrome" and throw myself at the foot of the cross and cry:

> *Forgive me, Father. Forgive me.*
> *Help my doubts and unbeliefs.*

I must choose then, to rest in the unmerited charity of God's forgiveness. I must choose to forgive myself for doubting the One Who is omniscient, omnipotent, omnipresent.

Natural eyes record generally. Spirit eyes record more precisely.

Holy. Holy. Holy.

III

THE FIVE SENSES

III

THE FIVE SENSES

*Never does the Word of God say to despise one's natural senses.
Discernment encompasses the use of both the
natural and spiritual giftings.*

Hearing, seeing, smelling, tasting, and touching are natural giftings that need to be employed in the arena of spiritual life. They assist in the realms of discerning, understanding. People assume they are disposable because they are not "spiritual," but this is far from the truth. We do not leave behind our bodies because they are not spirit. We are tripart—spirit, soul, body. All things work together.

On Heaven, Angels, and Jesus

I have seen angels. I have been in the presence of God's throne. As Paul would say, *whether out of or in my body, I do not know.* I have heard the voice of God that sounds like the many rushing waters, yet, gentle as a lamb, and I saw the reality of the Heavenly City from a distance. I have witnessed the blind see and the deaf hear and various and sundry other supernatural events that God Himself gives the command for.

Yet ...

I have known despair to the thought of suicide when young and concurrently a deep rage that simmered when life seemed vacant of hope ... not unlike others. I have experienced frugality to the point of not being able to afford a postage stamp and no place to call home but a park bench for a day. I have been subjected too often to a surgeon's knife. On the other hand, I have also been graced with sovereign deliverances from a cigarette habit, flu-like symptoms, and a simple headache when hands were laid on me and prayer offered on my behalf. I have been wrapped in wonderment, too, at the witnessing of many others' healings from small and great maladies, but also know the wrenching sorrow of a loved one's reaching their once appointed time to die.

I have known times of discrimination due to age and gender. I am familiar with deep woundings from the voices of friends and know the sting of character assassination. I have followed my heart, not to the sound of culture or of another's tradition, but to my own call and have been thought of as "trouble" due to my incessant questionings. I have been told to repent and turn when not able to embrace another's personal theological norm.

Back to Heaven, Angels, and Jesus

At the end of the day, what godly purpose is there to see angels or be shown a glimpse into heavenly realms and brought before the throne of grace? Certainly, it cannot be for personal gain or a sense of spiritual superiority. It cannot be that those experiences be shared as though they are merely for the asking. Scripture does not exhort disciples of Jesus to seek supernatural experiences, but God Himself. We are entreated to seek righteousness, peace, and joy in His Holy Spirit. We are to pick up our crosses, follow Him, and endure insults and losses of every kind. We are to exhibit love, even as He does.

But, if you happen to see an angel along the way, or hear the audible voice of God, or enter heaven for a glimpse, then magnificent. Just know it was not because of you, and do not bask in the glory as though it is yours. Receive from the experience and move on because building a tabernacle there will not enlarge the Kingdom in any way, but teaching Christ and Him crucified will.

Through it all like Paul

I am learning His ways slowly. I am knowing God's faithfulness and trusting more fully His presence and love. I am gaining, ever gradually, in contentment. I am struggling with the barrage of life's unknown factors, but less rigorously and more sporadically.

I am becoming, yes becoming, *more becoming* to my God.
That is more like the goal of our high calling, is it not?

And I hear the words of Paul in 1 Corinthians 13 from The Book:
*"There are three things that will endure—faith, hope and love—
and the greatest of these is love."*

*Today, I pray a sustaining faith as you wade through
the natural experiences of life, yet seek so much more …
I pray for you hope, just where you are in your journey with God.
I pray for you a greater awareness of the power of love.
And lastly and most importantly, I pray that you seek Jesus,
not an experience, for when you do, all of His Kingdom will be
opened onto you. His Word declares it so.*

68

Seeing Clearly?

*I*f there was a poll conducted around the world today, people would probably agree unanimously that *sight* is a most precious gift and would not easily entertain giving up their ability to see, even if offered grand sums of money. That is how prized the gift of physical sight truly is. It transcends even the spirit of greed and gain for most of humanity.

Not long ago, I had an interesting encounter with *sight* and *seeing*. Seated in a small portion of a room across from another person for about an hour, the time came to depart and go our separate ways. As we left the building and entered the parking area to finalize our goodbyes, I was inwardly astounded by what I was seeing. I realized only then what I did not see when seated so near earlier: I did not see the true color of the person's attire. What appeared indoors as an extremely pale crimson was, in fact, a true deep pink when brought into the fullness of a sunlit day.

For some, this event would be a non-event, and they would pass by it without another thought. To be unable see a color correctly is not cataclysmic. In fact, many experience this as their daily norm. We know them as color blind. But this is not my challenge, or I would be more readily able to accept the mis-seeing and move on without further exploration.

What could have happened in the natural when I did not see correctly that day if the issue presented had been of greater importance? In the right environment, a wrong conclusion based on a false premise may have destroyed a primary relationship, terminated employment, assassinated a reputation, incarcerated an innocent, or caused a life to be lost in surgery or a field of war. This error of sight could have had the potential to be as devastating as any tsunami. And in the spirit realm, the results may well be similar. Not seeing or perceiving truth may again result in broken relationships, unmet dreams, and deceptions of every kind. From Genesis through Revelation, the stories of the Bible explicitly deal with the consequences of mankind's mis-seeing or lack of perception. Kings lost their thrones, and others their rightful inheritances. Husbands were murdered, babies died, and women were sold into slavery because of it. Ultimately, one day, the lack of spiritual sight for some will find them forever separated from their Creator.

I had an awakening call that day by not seeing pink.
Consider taking time to ask God if you are seeing as He sees?
Then do according to your answer, as it just may color your world
differently, and the world of others profoundly.

On Daniel Chapter 5,
Is the Handwriting on the Wall?

*T*hese words, written so long ago, *Mene, Mene, Tekel, Upharsin,* that were manifested on King Belshazzar's palace wall the night of a tremendous gathering of royalty and festivity utilizing God's housewares in a merriment of gorging on fine food and wine, continue to carry instruction to us today. These words translated mean *"numbered, numbered, weighed, divisions."* And to the King, they were quite weighty and personal. So much so that they prophesied of his imminent death and the divisions of his kingdom on earth. For he did not learn from his father that hardness of heart, pride, and the worship of another God would not be tolerated by the Most High God.

When the King saw a part of a hand appear and a man's fingers write these words from out of nowhere, scripture tells us he turned color and all gaiety left him. Immediately, he called for all his wise men to come before him, and he offered them great wealth and position if they could interpret these four words to him with understanding; yet, they could not. At last, they called for Daniel, a man who was known for solving "knotty problems" and who was known as having a spirit of the Holy God within, as well as light and superior understanding and wisdom. And with Daniel came the answer to the trembling King and all his guests.

Daniel was not just any man with wisdom and insight, but the man appointed by God in that situation to have the divine wisdom and understanding needed for accuracy and truth.

On Counsel

Do you think it unreasonable to consider that God would use some people and some circumstances in your life in general ways and with general counsel. At other times, He would call for one, such as a Daniel who is filled with unusual light and wisdom, for a specific situation in a particular hour?

Have you always been able to read the writing on the wall in your own life circumstances or that of another? Could you have missed red flags of unheeded hunches? Have you ever refused the advice of counsel by summarily and abruptly dismissing it without consideration because it was contrary to your strongly-held belief on the issue or issues?

I put these simple thoughts and questions before you for your due diligence. Perhaps the questions are themselves your present-day handwriting on the wall.

Father God,
Cause us to be more sensitive to Your will and Your way. Help us forge our own rivers of prejudicial thoughts and ways so that we may find ourselves doing Your will. May we embrace Your servants as chosen for us, as you are a God of diversity and flavor. May we be like Daniel, people of great knowledge, wisdom, and people of discernment and usability, for the world needs just such.

Trains and The Wild West

*P*arallel to the highway for great amount of miles ran the tracks that would have gone unnoticed had it not been for the train's schedules matching ours.

The goods or the destination were not important to me. The train itself was the object of my curiosity. It was the perceived size of it that transfixed me.

We were in the Badlands of the West where dry, barren acres lay under the watchful peaks of mountains that stand at great distances away. The vastness of open range and open sky was exhilarating and welcoming after the suffocating busyness of the cities. Traveling from Los Angeles to Las Vegas to the Grand Canyon and back again was a delightful adventure, and trains played a major part as an object lesson.

When standing beside a train at a depot or sitting in a vehicle at a train crossing, one does not have to imagine the size or power of it. It is self-evident. Yet, put that same monstrous train against the landscape of the West and behold, it seems to be miniature and so diminutive you would think you were seeing a model train that may be found in any home under a Christmas tree or at a model railroad convention.

What is Your Reality?

It is this type of experience or *living example* that shouts: *things are not always what they seem!* My perceptions of the trains' sizes were an illusion, skewed by the distances, angles, and the actual dimensions of the objects.

Jesus, the Master of Truth, continues saying to those who are educated, intellectual, and well-appointed that things are not what they seem, always. Yet, eat, drink, and be merry today, for tomorrow will take care of itself. This is the unspoken mantra of old. Then, suddenly, a cyclone, a prominent leader is exposed for corruption, or a stock market crash occurs: One's reality is violently altered, at least for a sprint in time.

What is your reality today? The prophets cried for all to have ears to hear and eyes to see. Jesus Himself exhorted those within His fold, let alone those on the outside to have ears to hear and eyes to see. So, it is all about perception and perspective. *Perception* deceives, as the trip across the Badlands revealed. *Perspective*, too, will be flavored by the plumb line used. We must not forget this truth.

Wherever you are today, mentally, emotionally, physically, spiritually, and even geographically, right perspective is based on one thing and one thing alone. *Right* perspective is *His* perspective. Everything else is skewed.

The trains of the west … were they matchbox size or full-scale?

The Truth of any matter always sets us free. *I saw erroneously.* What may possibly require adjustment in your line of view? Ask for your needed present truth, and God will oblige you with His eternal omniscience. After all, we are His children, the sheep of His fold. It is His good pleasure to reveal.

May God richly imbue all with His sight.

Porch Sitt'n

*P*orch sitt'n is a phenomenon known almost exclusively to the people of the South, or, in the least, it can be said that Southerners seem to have an edge over others in the art of it. *Porch Sitt'n* is an old turn of phrase that describes what people have been doing for hundreds of years, sitting on their porches, sometimes alone, but most often with kin folk across the generations. This is where the old and new of every type of life incident was shared. Elders collectively framed family history, some true and some spun, neighbors were discussed, babies were rocked lovingly by old hands, and the young were set free to roam or hang on the porch rails to hear it all. Mostly, it was the way *to learn* one another. And to this day, it continues, with the added convenience of modern instruments filling the hands of the sitt'rs, much to the chagrin of the elders.

Much time has gone by since I was in the hills of Tennessee trying to locate an old friend. With the aid of a GPS system, I ended up at a wrong address way off the beaten path. To my astonishment, this home actually seemed to be placed smack in the middle of an animal pasture with a narrow road going through it. As I made my way to the house to ask for directions, there it was, this phenomenon called *porch sitt'n*. Four generations were rocking and talking together on that sunny day. And it took all four to discuss amongst themselves just where I might need to head to find my friend, and to do it before sundown, as many of the roads were unmarked and a stranger like myself would not be able to navigate well without the light of day. The three older generations could not specifically help, but they asked the younger if he thought his new type of phone could. And it did. Together, embracing the old and the new, they redirected this stranger in a harmony that I not only heard but felt within. They were one, even as they crossed the many natural years and technological advances that separated them.

As I made my way back to the path that was not oft beaten, where the speed, sounds, and sights of everything increased exponentially, I knew

75

God was talking. He is calling to His people to do some porch sitt'n. Porch sitt'n with Him first. Yes, we are being called back to the ancient art of listening, and in active purposed listening, we will find the knowing needed. In the knowing, we will find within it our fresh equipping. That is what God wants; He has always wanted it for His people. He wants to send His people who know Him, His ways, and His voice, to go porch sitt'n with those who do not know Him. It is effective. It is relational. It is evangelization. It is God.

Father, grace me, grace us collectively, to listen again for Your voice,
Your ways. Quiet us, so that we may hear anew,
as we porch sit with You for our good and the good of others.

Voices

*T*hese are true stories. The lessons to be learned are real.

There were four friends, all girls. One night, around one in the morning, they decided to go for a ride over the mountain to the neighboring state. Borrowing a car, without permission, off they went. With a fourteen-year-old at the wheel, a fifteen-year-old friend beside her, and two others in the back seat, these unlicensed teens engaged in banter. Then the lights and sirens interrupted their merriment. Police were in pursuit. Responding to this vehicle that was stolen and the lack of response to pull over, additional police were called and placed on alert that a speeding vehicle was entering into their neighboring town. As more police cars entered the chase, there still was no response from the girls' vehicle that, by now, had crossed the state line, exponentially increasing the charges to their crimes.

As the pursuit continued, the laughter within the vehicle subsided, and now the voices of three were vying for the driver's attention. The first voice shouted, "Go faster, go faster, go faster." The second piped in frantically and hollered, "Stop, stop, stop. Please stop." And to round out the litany of choice, the third voice entered the fray. She shouted at the top of her lungs from the back, "Just wreck the car. Kill us. We are in trouble. Kill us, please. We are in trouble." Indeed, they were in trouble!

Yet, by the grace of God, they were not killed, nor was anyone else hurt, though the potential for great harm to many was ever present as they sped through the night. Four young people's lives were drastically changed that day. They now had to deal with the voice of the law. No longer just teenagers, they were branded delinquents.

The girl's voices of the night now heard the voice of the law ...

Voices

In Africa, *the voices echoed,* "Pay him, Madam, just pay him." This mantra was in response to a young driver who demanded more money once en route, than the contract we agreed to. After all, he was in control, so he thought, as did the native pastors accompanying me. "Just pay him so we can get home. Pay him so we do not have to spend the night in the bush. Pay him." These voices of compromise rang louder as night began to creep in, and our circumstances of ease looked dimmer. Despite the possibilities of a long night, *these voices of pay from my host pastors were as offensive as the demand of a corrupt driver.*

I would not pay and could not because of conscience. To dance or compromise in this matter would equate to calling wrong right to a young man who needed to know a different way, not a cultural norm, and the no was not easily said as the outcome was unknown. *Obedience required the law this night.* Mercy was not warranted. They had to deal with the voice of the law, and it was *no to more money.* Surprisingly, the trip resumed quietly for the ride out of the bush and into the city with the rescinding of the unscrupulous driver's demand.

Voices of the night now heard the voice of the law ...

Voices, there are many. As we journey forward, may we do it with renewed courage and humility, determined to hear as well as respond, to what the Spirit has to say in all facets of our lives.

Though there will always be competing sounds or voices of opinion, we must discern, discriminate, and differentiate them as we seek God alone. It is an exercise for the mature. It is a call.

God says to His people, if you knock, ask, and seek in earnest, a response will be given. And if the way specified seems less than smooth, take comfort, for He also said through the Prophet Isaiah:

When you pass through the waters, I will be with you;
And through the rivers, they will not overflow you.
When you walk through the fire, you will not be scorched,
Nor will the flame burn you.
                                                —Isaiah 43:2 (NASB)

The Grasshopper Within

hen Caleb quieted the people before Moses and said, "We should by all means go up and take possession of it, for we will certainly prevail over it." But the men who had gone up with him said, "We are not able to go up against the people, because they are too strong for us." So they brought a bad report of the land which they had spied out to the sons of Israel, saying, "The land through which we have gone to spy out is a land that devours its inhabitants; and all the people whom we saw in it are people of great stature. We also saw the Nephilim there (the sons of Anak are part of the Nephilim); and we were like grasshoppers in our own sight, and so we were in their sight."

—Numbers 13:30-33 (NASB)

And What Do You See?

*"... and we were like grasshoppers in our own sight,
and so we were in their sight."*

This simple phrase may be one of the most dangerous and destructive statements we can make in Kingdom living when applied by the natural mind. With repetition of statements, thought patterns emerge that can become equal to or greater than the Word of God. We then find ourselves navigating through life, not as we are in Christ, but as we define ourselves in comparison to others and the circumstances we find ourselves in. What do you see, a tugboat or a ship: A huge ship that will swamp the little tug, or a tug rightly fitted with enough power and size to guide the mighty ship out into the sea? Do you see a tiny tug at the mercy of a vast body of water, or a toy-like boat in a contained tub of water?

Right Perspective Equals No Comparisons

We must learn from Numbers 13. The Israelites were seen by others not as they were but as they perceived themselves to be. Let us not sin, in like kind. We must see as God sees, and He sees us not in comparison to our brothers, sisters, mothers, fathers, friends, or mentors but as individual, unique creations. Let us not compare country against country, skin tone to skin tone, or dialect to dialect. Let us not compare profession against profession, church to church, nor bank account to bank account, for when we do, we lose perspective and receive to ourselves less than or more than truth. It is not God's way.

What do you see and feel when you look in the mirror of your life?
Does it align with God's version?

We must recognize and consciously turn away from the grasshopper mentality found in our thinking. When God instructs and directs, we are quite able, quite able to realize the goal … Watchman Nee said, "Seeing is deliverance."

Father God, cause us then to see, so we may be free.

The Winds of March

John 15

*M*arch in the natural: It is almost unnecessary to look at the calendar; just step outside. The air is being stirred. Trees, young and old alike, are creaking as they sway to and fro as some of their limbs are being strewn here and there. Discarded odds and ends from uncaring motorists are flipping and skipping down the highways and byways. An uprooting and replacing of objects is in process by the very winds of March.

As I left the shelter of my home with my dog, she heard and felt the winds of March and, tucking her tail, lunged for the door. Fear struck her. The sights and sounds of March were quite clearly unnerving. The stirring of the wind and the reordering of debris about the grounds were intolerable. If she could speak the language of people, I could imagine her saying, "No, no, and no. I do not like these changes. Things are not as they are to be, nor how they were." The quietude and placement of the old is comforting. Are these thoughts familiar?

Jesus suggested in His Word that nature reveals the times, and if we are wise, we will see and hear what is transpiring in the Spirit? The actions of the winds of March by the Spirit may be at hand but do not fear the process of your thoughts, reasonings, and imaginations being uprooted and reorganized. Do not fight the blowing and re-syncing work of the Holy Spirit in this season of your life. Mature as the old creaking trees. They learned to bend with the winds, for in bending, one does not break.

Your assignment, and mine, in our ordained seasons of March, whenever it manifests, is to trust God during the pruning process. Remember, even as nature, we need to be pruned back for growth.

Peace, peace to those who are in process, in Christ.

Being Shod, Equipping

*S*hoes are interesting, at least to some people and less to others, as is everything under the sun. My attention was drawn to my shoes one day as I sat in a friend's home with my feet propped up, by invitation. I had on a pair of old sandals, and the lack of a sole struck me. Literally, the bottoms of my sandals were worn smooth.

It Just Happened?

The lack of soles on my sandals caused me to look at other things in my life, including my car tires, soon thereafter. I was shocked at what I saw, and it was confirmed by my mechanic. My tires were no better off than my shoes. The tread was unmistakably worn to a place of potential danger. In the natural, without exaggeration, the worn conditions of both my sandals and tires could have led to bodily and property injury.

We often hear, *it just happened!* However, upon further investigation, a different picture frequently emerges. My worn-out sandals did not just happen in one day. The principle of use commenced immediately when I began wearing them. The circumstances of weather, times worn, and the surfaces the soles were subjected to, day in and day out, had an effect and were cumulative over time.

In truth, what happened at my friend's house was that I was put in the right position to see.

Thank God nothing serious took place when I was walking or driving. The potential for harm was there because the conditions of wear and tear altered the once safe, usable originals.

You may be thinking, *this is such a small matter it is not worthy of even a mention.* But consider …

The Spiritual Parallel
Put On The Full Armor Of God

Throughout the Word of God, we are entreated to be alert and aware of the times and seasons we are living in. The Apostle Paul in Ephesians tells us to put on the full armor of God.

Ephesians 6:11-18 (NASB) states, *"Put on the full armor of God, so that you will be able to stand firm against the schemes of the devil. For our struggle is not against flesh and blood, but against the rulers, against the powers, against the world forces of this darkness, against the spiritual forces of wickedness in the heavenly places. Therefore, take up the full armor of God, so that you will be able to resist on the evil day, and having done everything, to stand firm. Stand firm therefore, having belted your waist with truth, and having put on the breastplate of righteousness, and having strapped on your feet the preparation of the gospel of peace; in addition to all, taking up the shield of faith with which you will be able to extinguish all the flaming arrows of the evil one. And take the helmet of salvation and the sword of the Spirit, which is the word of God. With every prayer and request, pray at all times in the Spirit, and with this in view, be alert with all perseverance and every request for all the saints ..."*

This instruction of equipping is to always be in the present tense, so that we live in a state of preparedness. An equipped soldier is *not necessarily* a prepared soldier. The soles of my sandals and tread of my tires are testimony to this truth. My *shoddings* were woefully inadequate for offensive or defensive maneuvers. *In the natural*, they had surpassed their usefulness and needed replacement.

Again, First in the Natural, Then in The Spirit

Considering this word, these questions arise. Are we fully dressed in the prescribed spiritual armor needed for this hour? Is the condition of our armor ready for battle? If the answer is no, and we are not equipped, our usefulness is woefully diminished for assignments in the Kingdom of God. To march forward, preparation is key. Think on this.

The Word

I am hungry. My appetite has been increasing as the weather begins to change, I have noticed. As I find myself reaching here, there, and everywhere for something to nibble on, a quiet, unobtrusive thought floats through me in the form of a question. What is it I am really in want of? What is it that will satisfy, which my nibbling has not? I conclude... it has nothing to do with natural but rather spirit sustenance. I am in need of more of The Word. In response, I choose the topic of love to nourish and rediscover. For some it is a familiar passage, other's perhaps not. But who of us does not need to be reminded of what love is genuinely about?

Love Never Grows Old

The Way of Love

If I speak with human eloquence and angelic ecstasy but don't love, I'm nothing but the creaking of a rusty gate. If I speak God's Word with power, revealing all his mysteries and making everything plain as day, and if I have faith that says to a mountain, "Jump," and it jumps, but I don't have love, I'm nothing.

If I give everything I own to the poor and even go to the stake to be burned as a martyr, but don't love, I've gotten nowhere. So no matter what I say, what I believe, and what I do, I'm bankrupt without love.

Love never gives up.
Love cares more for others than for self.
Love doesn't want what it doesn't have.
Love doesn't strut,
Doesn't have a swelled head,
Doesn't force itself on others,
Isn't always "me first,"
Doesn't fly off the handle,

Doesn't keep score of the sins of others,
Doesn't revel when others grovel,
Takes pleasure in the flowering of truth,
Puts up with anything,
Trusts God always,
Always looks for the best,
Never looks back,
But keeps going to the end.

Love never dies. Inspired speech will be over some day; praying in tongues will end; understanding will reach its limit. We know only a portion of the truth, and what we say about God is always incomplete. But when the Complete arrives, our incompletes will be canceled.

When I was an infant at my mother's breast, I gurgled and cooed like any infant. When I grew up, I left those infant ways for good.

We don't yet see things clearly. We're squinting in a fog, peering through a mist. But it won't be long before the weather clears, and the sun shines bright! We'll see it all then, see it all as clearly as God sees us, knowing him directly just as he knows us!

But for right now, until that completeness, we have three things to do to lead us toward that consummation: Trust steadily in God, hope unswervingly, love extravagantly. And the best of the three is love.

—1 Corinthians 13:1-13 (MSG)

God's Definition of Love

May we run to Him when our natural appetites are crying out,
demanding more flesh, the flesh of others ...

Fan, Kindle, Stir:
There's a Job to be Done

That is why I remind you to fan into flame the gracious gift of God, [that inner fire—the special endowment] which is in you through the laying on of my hands [with those of the elders at your ordination].
                                                    —2 Timothy 1:6 (AMP)

There is no doubt what the Apostle Paul was instructing his young protégé, Timothy, to be doing. There was a job before him to accomplish for Christ, and he needed to be prepared.

Not long ago, at a prayer meeting, a reminder came forth from God to "ignite and re-ignite" in the spirit, for He wanted to use this group to bring forth the gifts of His Spirit for the fulfillment of the new vision. Most present were already learned in such things. Why the need for this word?

Possibly, it hinged on God's intimate knowledge of His creation's short memory span and the forever need to nudge both the natural and spirit man forward for the facilitation of the intended purpose. Like a coach coming alongside fatigued athletes in training, his/her voice is to encourage and prod them on to the goal, as is the one sent to fan and stir. Maximizations in the natural and spirit realms can only be engaged in for limited durations before a renewed source of energy is needed to be tapped into. Coaches know their athletes thoroughly and create plans, sequences, and times for rest, refueling, and acceleration. God does, too.

It is incumbent upon all who are running the race for Christ to be alert to His voice declaring "fan, flame, rekindle, sit, stay, or shake the dust off."

The choice of message or messenger is not ours to pick or choose from like a buffet. This is solely God's domain, and we must embrace this truth if we are to be more usable.

I want to be readily usable, and so I will thank Him for these reminders, believing His purpose is far greater and grander than my imagining. I choose to fan, flame, and re-ignite afresh my inner fire. It must be in need, for God sent the word and confirmed it.

And you? Any recent reminders to fan, kindle, stir?

I Dreamed,
The Labyrinth

I dreamed this dream. I do not often remember dreams, nor do I seek them. Nevertheless, I did, and it was memorable not because it was of great grandeur but because of its profound simplicity.

The dream began in an underground setting. When I arrived in this massive sub-earth environment, I was met by several individuals who were unknown to me and two who were close and trusted loved ones. Like any underground infrastructure that holds the mechanical underpinnings for modern life such as the plumbing, furnaces, boilers, wiring, etc., it was less than remarkable. The rooms were many and vast, with much diverse activity within, but they were alike in the sense the surroundings made me feel inwardly uncomfortable, although I did not know why. Was it simply a reaction to the clamor and the grindings being emitted from the assortment of machinery within this semi-dim environment, or maybe the feverishness of the activities being performed? My wonderings were many, but nothing in the natural seemed out of order, so I continued the walk-through with my hosts. At first, not much was being said, but eventually the conversation began to enlarge on their part. I simply was looking and listening but not speaking as different people conversed with me about various issues. Interestingly, they did not engage my accompanying blood relatives. They seemed just to be there for initial legitimacy reasons. My uncomfortableness never left but remained as we journeyed on together.

Suddenly, I had what I will call a flash of light, a flash of truth that pierced through my inner consciousness illuminating to me that what was being said and done, how things were being portrayed and appeared *were not the way things were*. This flash aligned with my inner discomfort that I had been experiencing since my arrival.

The flash of understanding, in a miniscule measurement of time, was both present and absent, much like a burst of lightning. But, and nevertheless, we all continued through the labyrinth of the underground structure eventually arriving at the above ground level.

On the surface once again, I found myself in unusually striking physical surroundings. The stunningly beautiful vast building complex encircled by lush forests was finished in exquisite natural wood and was linked by a system of walkways that were just as appetizing to the naked eye. The structures seemed to be like condominiums or townhouses that were of varying sizes and heights, each unique, each stately, each standing alone yet connected. As I was being guided through and around this immense compound, the farther we went the more pleasurable and lovely it was. The exquisiteness of the craftsmanship was visually astounding.

Simultaneously with all my delight I became aware: *The farther away I got in time and place from the revealing flash of truth that all was not as it seemed, the dimmer it got.* It was as though the truth was being covered up and swallowed up by what I continued to be subjected to visually and auditorily. What I was presently seeing, feeling, and hearing in the natural was trumping and trumped the spirit revelation that things were not as they seemed.

And I *willfully chose* to lay aside the insight given in favor of and for the pleasure of the moment and its unfolding experience, whatever that was to be.

I ask, how often have you done the same?
This dream … is a teaching of profound simplicity.
Will the warning chimes of the Spirit within be heeded?

IV

CROSS CULTURAL

Red, Yellow, Brown, Black, White,
Rural, City

IV

CROSS CULTURAL:

Red, Yellow, Brown, Black, White, Rural, City

*Understanding God's ways experientially versus academically
is a journey with the Holy Spirit that will humble the proud
and set firm foundations.*

*N*o, it was never my intention, nor ever on my internal radar screen to go to Africa, Asia, or Europe. And especially not to do missions. Although many dream this dream, it was not mine.

However, sitting in my local church one day, a word came forth: "You, in the blue and white striped sweater. Yes, you. You are going to have zeal increase to go out and do the things of the Lord. You are going not just here but other countries. Put that in your back pocket and take it before the Lord." And, in due season, that became my reality.

I acknowledge the beauty and the need by design of cross pollination in the natural and spirit. Bridges form, walls tumble down, and greater understandings sprout forth concerning differing cultural expressions of all things. We can learn of and from one another if we are open.

As I continue to walk, I am ever learning of God's ways and, as a disciple, ever desiring to shun the comfortableness of conformity and embrace diversity, while remaining in unity when there is no contradiction to the intent of the Word of God.

I have been immeasurably enriched because of my yes to the calls to go to other nations. Mission work is life challenging and life changing. I have found that to see, to hear, to smell, to touch, is to better understand.

For those who have been called to other nations long term, I bow my knee. It is sacrificial.

The Bag Lady of Philly

*A*few years after accepting the Lord, I was in Philadelphia, Pennsylvania, for missions training in preparation for months of life and ministry in Sweden. In conjunction with classroom instruction, a practical outreach had to be chosen. I decided to be a part of a team that went into the inner city to prepare and paint the walls of the interior of a building that was abandoned and condemned but was now being renovated for the homeless. This was *doing* the gospel, and it felt so good.

One day after painting and in route back to our own beautifully restored campus, we stopped at a corner grocery, near the future shelter, to pick up a snack.

I vividly remember getting my drink and a pack of crackers, paying for them, and then beginning to move towards the door to leave. Just as I began to turn the corner, I was startled by the presence of a person directly in my path. She was not of large stature, but instantly and literally, she was in my face and said, "Give me a cracker." I do not fully recollect what hit me first: The stench, the tone, the sound of a crackling voice or her overall appearance. Her hair was indescribably matted, and her baggy holey clothes were hanging on her frame as though tossed on, by the wind. Her sneakers were of the same caliber. In her weathered hands and hanging by her side, were two bags of what I assumed were her earthly possessions. And then, as if she thought I did not hear her the first time, she rapidly repeated her desire for a cracker.

Outwardly and consciously, I graciously responded to her desire. Inwardly, I recoiled and was repulsed from the presence of her being and touch. Simultaneously, I was smitten by the Word of God and reminded that the very mission I was undertaking was for the many like her, the homeless in spirit. Those seconds, which seemed like an eternity, ended as quickly as they began.

Or did they?

It has been many years, but the sights, sounds, and odors of my Bag Lady of Philadelphia have never left me. She continues to go where I go.

As we often read in scripture, the "and suddenly" encounter was upon me, and it shook me to the core of my being. Inwardly ashamed and downcast from my reaction, I quietly rejoined my group to go back to suburbia and middle-class America for the evening.

Where my lady went, I will never know. Perhaps she found shelter that night under a bridge or maybe she was warmed by a city grate or even by a cardboard box that so many people, even in America, call home.

Had it not been for the incredibly wise mentor God had placed in my life years before for coaching and accountability, I may not have negotiated this giant exposure of self-life, still present in me, right before the launching of my first mission assignment.

I felt useless and un-usable. I was horrified at my repulsion of another human being. And I was to be a carrier of the Good News to another nation? What hypocrisy!

A simple statement of truth delivered in due season brought the freedom and courage needed to continue walking on. Hope abounded and truth set me free when Jeannine, my mentor, quietly stated: *"Mother Teresa's are not born, but rather are made, as is every other disciple of Jesus Christ. Be assured,"* she said, *"God will give you another opportunity to see His hand of sanctification and the emergence of His Spirit within you. Ask forgiveness, and be at rest."*

With due repentance and asking for forgiveness of God, His peace immediately flooded my mind, will, and emotions. And, in time, I could forgive myself. Since those many years ago of facing my own flesh, I have been able to extend the same wise counsel to others knowing they too would be restored.

May we in turn pay forward all things good …

Redemption Three Years Later, From Bag Lady to Hobo

A friend asked me if I would be willing to accompany her to see her youngest son graduate from military training. I had the time, and we confirmed a date.

God uses our differences

The trip would be long, and in response, my friend packed lunches for both of us. That is not something I would normally or otherwise do, as I have an intense dislike for car dining, unless on a train. However, it was done, and we were on our way.

With many miles behind us as we entered the State of Georgia, it seemed a perfect time for a rest stop and to change drivers. It was in this process that my redemption drew near.

I was now in the driver's seat and alone when I heard a tapping on the window. As I turned to respond to the tapping, what met my gaze was a toothless, hairy, and slightly bent over man grinning from ear to ear. The window was slightly cracked, and through it, he told me he was hungry and asked softly if I had anything to eat. With the initial shock of his presence behind me, not his disheveled, craggy appearance or his impoverished lean-looking body, but just his sudden appearance beside me, I was free to respond with the true, gracious love of a child of God. With every fiber of my being, I wanted to reach out and meet his very real and present need from a heart engorged with kindness.

He was welcome to all that my friend had packed. It was for the asking. We had other resources, and I knew she would affirm my decision.

God had worked His wonder. Within my once dark soul, He quietly and imperceptibly had created His Christlikeness in me in a way and measure I was not cognizant of.

My mentor was right. No surprise really, as she has walked the trail as a wise woman of God for scores of years. It happened, as she said. God would redeem my bag-lady encounter in His time and in His way. She did not know when or how, only that He would be faithful to my heart's cry for change and its need for transformation.

Yes. This is right perspective.

God does use and continues to call the imperfect. I am one with the Apostle Paul when he proclaimed the sense of being chief amongst sinners. *But for the grace of God* is a phrase we often parrot, but this is the whole truth.

God is making us, fear not the process.
He is able. We will stumble. Yet, he is able.
Are there any Bag Ladies or Hobos in your closet?
God is able, I know.

And finally, my mentor's wisdom, like Solomon's, continues to be my heart's desire. The giftings of God are for the preeminent purpose of passing them forward for the keeping of others in times of testing. She did not with-hold God's gift of truth to me. We must always remember that only truth will set any one of us free.

Why Go To Africa,
Frank Asked

*S*ome time ago, I engaged in a conversation with a gentleman from Ireland who has made the United States his home for forty plus years. An engineer by profession, he was interested in how a rock-climbing piece of equipment worked at the physical therapy-wellness center. I received the question because I happened to be beside his station, throwing a ball against a small trampoline at the time. I had never seen him before although both of us had been attending for rehab purposes for quite some time. After a brief introduction to one another's lives, we found the *heart-beat* of our meeting. And *it was God*. He was intrigued with my line of work as a single female in ministry. He had been a Presbyterian Sunday School Superintendent many, many years ago while still in his homeland.

Life continued, but without God, until the week before we met. Frank shared that he had just attended the funeral of the man who opened the door to him in America and was astonished by the joy of the service. He acknowledged the beauty of it, and what a curiosity it was now that the same life in death, was causing him to re-look at his belief system that once embraced the God of Christianity, at least in theory.

Frank was now apprehensive. He said he did not know how to talk to God anymore as it had been so long. Would God even remember him? If God did, he was still apprehensive about coming to Him so late in his life. He thought it was as usury, and it did not settle well. Wasn't it too late perhaps for the relationship to be genuine? Anyway, who was he to think God would even be interested in him anymore. But he said, "I have been a good man. I have harmed no one, and I have shared with the underprivileged."

And then it was my turn to speak. His small, fixed, blue Irish eyes were moistened as he gave me his full attention, and I called him back to the days when he was fresh, probing, and open to believing God was Who He said He was. Layer after layer of the clouds of life and man's indoctrinations were being peeled away ever so slowly. Chip, chip, chip went the words against his thoughts. It was as though I could see the machinations of his thought processes being eroded right before me, with the simple truth of God's continued love for this set of Irish eyes. I sensed the open window of free communication was folding. But before it was closed, I had one more clear unction.

By the way, Frank, you do not have to worry anymore of how you can re-approach God. He knows me quite well, and I am going to let Him know today that a newfound friend of mine that goes by the name of Frank, an old friend of His, will soon be in touch.

And To Answer The Question Posed: Why go to Africa?

As assuredly as I had a divine Saturday appointment at a wellness center on a sunny afternoon in America with God's Irish transplanted son, Frank, I have some ordained dates in Africa.

No, Frank, I cannot stay home, but you cannot understand this now.

Who will go? I must go. God is calling. I can hear him clearly. There are many more Franks, and they live in Africa. I must go.

As I was writing this, I stopped to hear the words of a tune playing softly on the radio in the background. This is what I heard:

> "Speak, Lord, for your servant listens.
> Show me where to go. Tell me what to say.
> Light my path, point the way.
> Yes, Lord, your command is heard.
> Yes, Lord, I obey your word."

> "Mold me as a useful vessel in your hand.
> I do not ask for riches; I do not ask for fame
> Or honor to be heaped on my name.
> I ask your presence …
> Speak, Lord, for your servant hears."

Thanks, God. I get it.

A Perspective,
Neither All Black Nor All White

- She said, "Whose time are we going to be on today, African time or God's time?"
- He said, "African time. Have you ever thought about why we are late?"
- "Maybe because it takes two hours to gather the charcoal needed to cook, and then it takes additional time to flame the fire to get it to ignite?"
- "Maybe because we must go to the field to pick the dinner potatoes and get home again?"
- "Maybe because we must navigate very, very, very bad roads?"
- "Maybe because the cars are not so good?"
- "Maybe we are late due to the lack of sun needed to dry our clothes?"
- "Maybe because of a lot of such things you do not have to deal with?"
- After some consideration, she said, "But, brother, when was the last time you experienced any of the above that caused you to be late?"
- And then there was silence.

These are illuminating tensions in cross cultural exchanges.

God and Inconvenient Truths

*W*hen the culture of Western proficiency with miniscule tolerance for excuses and many of the citizens of laid back third world culture who lack access to various modern conveniences meet, tensions rise. The gulf that lies between the two in experience and expectation is so wide one is left to wonder: just who is right. Once one personally gets beyond who is right concerning the issue, the corresponding question becomes whose side is God on. When the ways of His people clash, truth is about to be revealed, for His Word says correction begins in the house/people of the Lord.

Truth is inconvenient at times, is it not? Have you ever been fulfilling your daily routine when the still small voice of adjustment interjects with an unannounced visit? Remember still and small does not equate to lack of importance, for when the voice of God calls, out of bounds, it is precisely the right time to say, "Yes, Lord, I am listening," and immediately forgo whatever is at hand. If we adhere to the belief that God is sovereign and therefore always timely, we must conclude that although His attendance seems inconvenient in the natural, it cannot be in spiritual concerns.

Again she asks, but this time to herself: *whose time will we be on, Africans' again or God's.*

Then the voice of a Righteous Mediator is heard saying ...

Daughter from the West: I want you to know again my heart of compassion, and I am doing it by your personal exposure to the daily hardships in the lives of others. The underlying reasons for lateness can be legitimate. Can't you see? Truth without context is uncompromisingly harsh, and it is not my way.

Son of the Third World: I want you to know the relevance and honor of timeliness. A people are known by their word, and the progress you long for comes with discipline. You know there are times when irritation and disturbance is an appropriate response. Don't you agree? Excuses offered, no matter how legitimate, devoid of disciplines, are not true excuses and are not My way.

And so, we return to where we began. Most issues of life are neither all black nor all white. There are many gray areas and interpretations. We differ while on earth, but we must come to recognize an eternal truth that our interpretation will never alter God's written word.

Perspective counts. Whose side is God on anyway? His and hers. Yes, his and hers. Are you listening?

If anyone has ears to hear, let him hear.
—Mark 4:23

Be thankful, for God's mercies are new to each one of us every morning.
—*Lamentations 3: 22-23*

Everything Has Ears, Kenya

Back to Basics

*H*ave you ever heard a statement that you are certain you heard before but evidently really did not *hear*? I say evidently because when we truly *hear*, most often, there is an atmosphere of immediacy in a response, which would be appropriate. Truth demands a reaction.

I heard while in Africa, "All things have ears"

It was as though I had been hit with a torpedo between my eyes and the ensuing explosion ripped through every *hearing fiber* of my being. The swiftness and intensity of the messaging word arrived and was delivered in such a way that there was no doubt God was speaking to me. The sound was deafening, and the purpose calls me to awaken. *Awaken sleeper. Awaken to the sound of your own voice. Take inventory. What are you saying? What are you speaking? When and for what purposes are you lending your voice?*

In my stillness, all I can hear is …

God, in the beginning, *said*, let there be light, and there was light.
God *said* to the waters divide and to the mountains stand, and it was so.
Joshua and the others *shouted*, and the walls of Jericho tumbled down.
Elijah *commanded* the rain to cease, and the rain ceased.
Elisha *said* live and the young boy came back to life.
Peter and John *said* to the lame man, walk, and he walked.
Jesus *said* to the fig tree, wither, and it withered.
Jesus *said* to the hand of a man, grow out. It responded accordingly.
Jesus *said* to waves and wind, be still. Calm ensued.
Jesus *said* to demons, leave the man and enter the pigs. They fled.

On and on go the biblical accounts threaded throughout the Old and

New Testaments of natural elements, animals, and insects of every living variety and kind, as well as human beings and human limbs *hearing* and then *responding* to the vocal commands given through God and man. We speak when we believe. However, God corrects the order; *hear first, then speak what you have heard. In essence, what we hear we respond to.*

The Word of God records, and life suggests just that;
all things have ears.
If true, what are the people and circumstances
in your life hearing via your voice?
What is God hearing? Worth pondering?

If Jesus Says Yes, Uganda

*T*here is a song that goes, *"If Jesus say yes, nobody can say no,"* that I heard while in Africa. It could not have sounded more beautiful if heavenly angels heralded it themselves. The exquisitely lush mountains, yet economically destitute area of Uganda was a magnificent place on earth for me to hear.

The echo continues within my soul, *If Jesus say yes, nobody can say no*. Repeatedly, the little song presents itself, beckoning me to embrace it and to entrust the Holy Spirit with breaking this truth open, in new and unimaginable ways. While in Africa, I heard it as a signal to trumpet repeatedly for the natives to not let their natural poverty or dearth rule and reign upon them. Rather, they were to take hold of the entire God-given potential within and reach long for all the possibilities without. Other nations did just that, and Africans as well can continue to build upon their natural and spiritual resources. May they learn from others' missteps, and may they mature in ways Western nations have not.

Yes, to what God says yes to. Unlike third world nations, the West has so much more materially, yes, even the least of us. As a people and as a society, we have become so inclusive of philosophies and religions to be so politically correct we have wandered away from our principled foundations and are summarily excluding God. We must return, individually and collectively, and voice "no" to what God says no to irrespective of consequences. Painfully, it begins within each of us. Let God freely examine all that you are, all that you have, all that you think, all that you do.

Do we have the fortitude to say yes to God and no to man?
If Jesus say yes, nobody can say no.

Let us move forward. We are not third world in the natural. But they are not third world in the spirit. Who is impoverished? Many, many Africans are rich in spirit. God did say, the poor in spirit will find. Industrialized and post-industrialized nations are destitute in a vastly different manner than Africa. It is time to acknowledge the circumstances. It is time for change.

If Jesus say yes, nobody can say no.
It is a banner worthy to be waved and as a song to be lived
by all people, tribes, tongues, male and female alike ...

How Beautiful Are His Feet, Tanzania

*G*eorge is his name. Pastor George. A native of Tanzania, East Africa. I first laid eyes on Pastor George when he was ministering the gospel at an outdoor crusade. His relatively short physical stature was overshadowed by a kinetic mental and spiritual exuberance far exceeding most ministers riding an evangelistic circuit. This man exuded a spirit of inviting love, as he called to those still entrenched in the fields of the world's sin.

His brown skin tones shone ever brighter under the late day sun and the deep pink dress shirt illumined him even more. But as my eyes surveyed this charismatic man from head to foot, the cause of his extremely hobbled cadence was not identifiable from a distance. And it was the distinct hobble that seemed incongruent with the high verbal and physical movement before the sea of faces, including mine. Intrigue set in. As I watched this man physically covering the platform from side to side for a good length of time and then finally step down rather precariously from the elevated platform, I knew I needed to know more. And so, I asked, and then I saw. As the pastor-evangelist slowly and methodically lifted his dress pants, the cause of the hobble was graphically witnessed. Before me, in the natural, I saw two extremely deformed feet encased in specially-fitted, soft, leather-like wraps resembling shoes. He said nothing. I said nothing. But the third person's voice who was present was emphatically clear. God said: "How beautiful are his feet." Inwardly, I stared. Immediately, I thanked George for allowing me a literal glimpse into his natural story for greater understanding.

How beautiful are his feet? Is this what his mother saw at birth, siblings, school-aged friends, and George himself as he passed through each developmental stage of growth? His church? His colleagues? And now his own children? Do they see beauty? I do not know. I cannot say, but I do know my natural man at first saw a radiance, a beauty about this man, and then I did not. Initially, what I saw was a handsome charismatic man with an unusual gait until his trousers were lifted. Suddenly, the unusual morphed to deformity and, again, I briefly redefined the whole man, for I saw him in part. He became his deformed feet. But God intervened. He caused me to see as He sees. And what He sees is beautiful. He sees a man in his image. A man, who in spite of a natural challenge, who could have succumbed to a picture of being egregiously crippled, but did not, rose to his full stature, embraced himself, and said, "I can, I am, and I will."

Evangelist George's yes and my yes met briefly in a city named Dar es Salaam. I am the richer. For I have been granted eyes to see here and now, as a young woman twenty plus years ago saw, when she said, "I Do, to the then young George."

May all our spirit eyes be opened. It is our Father's heart.

Going Fishing, India

"*O*nce again, writing to you … Will you consider going with us in prayer and material support?

We are going fishing. We are fishing for those who need to know Jesus, and fishing for those who know Him but are cold. We will be fishing for those who are hungry for more of Him and those who are broken in spirit, soul, and body.

Going fishing in the name of Jesus and our thanks is to God for those who go with us by way of prayer and material support.

Together, we will be effective in the land of India, for such a time as this. And together we will give thanksgiving to God for the things He ordained to accomplish through our simple act of obedience.

The fruit of the righteous is a tree of life. He who is wise wins souls.
—Proverbs 11:30 (AMP)

Back from Fishing

Writing to you once more. Please know God did more than we could ask or think. To name a few: People were born again, enlarging His Kingdom. Tormented minds were made to be at peace. Deaf ears were opened. A blind eye saw. A documented heart condition was healed. A drunk was sobered instantaneously while leaning on our ministry van when he heard the Good News.

Are you certain of these things? Yes. They personally said so. Their pastors said so. We simply listened …

He sent us. Two in the natural. All of you from Home. And God had His will and way …

We say thank you, and heaven rejoices.
Obedience is Key.

Acke in Sweden, Dead in Four Days

*T*his is a memory that should never be forgotten, has not been, nor could ever be. It is a weighty life memory, a memory that had a dire consequence and continues to live.

Many years ago, when on a missionary journey to northern Sweden, a young team, in which I was part, descended into a beautiful land with an assignment to teach English, share the gospel, and present cross-cultural public presentations. And this is how Acke of Sweden became my lifelong teacher.

We were introduced in the teachers' lounge on our first day. Classroom assignments had been predetermined by the administration and my lot was to teach with Acke. He was a quiet and intense intellectual, esteemed by those he worked with. I found him to be just such a man in the brief three days we walked together. His questioning was lively, open ended, intense, intentional, and spanned multi-dimensions of political, philosophical, spiritual, and cultural differences between the Swedish and American systems. And it was the spiritual issues of life and death that we conversed about privately between class instruction. I knew God. Acke was seeking. And only God, only God held the knowledge of the fourth day as well as the first.

It was on the fourth day that teacher Acke, also an avid outdoorsman was found lifeless, slumped under a tree with a rifle by his side. Most thought a senseless tragic accident occurred. However the official cause of death was deemed a suicide. The community at large was stunned, and yet, for me, Ackes' intense God-probing questions of day one, two, and three, a foretelling. In hindsight, the answer seemed self-evident, and because of this, my life was altered.

Back now to the first day. As with any team, variety exists, and this truth became glaringly obvious and was as stark as night and day. Out of a team of five, only one broke rank with the given mission philosophy of building intentional relationships first and only then share the Christian faith. David's breaking with accepted protocol and what is often perceived as good manners that initial day was the lone voice that may have had eternal consequences. He boldly and unabashedly proclaimed the Good News of Jesus' death, burial, and resurrection, and the consequence of eternal separation from God, according to Christian tenets, to the teachers present in the room. The perceived shame and angst of the remaining team members, including myself, on that first day was swallowed up and annihilated by death itself. David's boldness in hindsight seemed self-evident. His spirit-voice was used contrary to the majority's, in which I was complicit in silence. He was an evangelist, not bound by nor under the restraint of man's protocol.

My life was forever changed. *I was sobered.* Four days in Sweden with a dynamic educator named Acke I pray will remain an ever-alive teaching.

May we all be more courageous.

Remember that neither etiquette nor the majority should ever rule when God says speak.

V

CLASSICS
Teachings that Stand the Test of Time

V

CLASSICS
Teachings that Stand the Test of Time

Never does the Word of God say to despise one's natural senses.
Discernment encompasses the use of both the
natural and spiritual giftings.

*P*rinciples.

I believe the following Mini's identify a variety of scenarios that are so common to mankind that we can clearly see the repetitive nature in them from generation to generation. No, we may not personally experience each of the classics, but again, if we are even minimal observers of life, we will come to know of the principles as watchers of others. And as disciples, whether young or more mature in the philosophies and tenets of God, the opportunity exists to be ever learning, ever challenged …

Pap's Wisdom

By JLM

*I*t was a blistering hot day in the lowlands when our family decided to go higher into the mountains for a refreshing early eve swim. Pap and Uncle packed as many kids as possible in the old car and off we went in the tin bucket on wheels. Reaching our destination, we unloaded gaily and ran toward and into the coolness immediately. But our frolicking in the chilly mountain water was cut short by a carload of others' arrival.

It happened once before. I knew the drill. We were all called out of the water for this small band of people to do a baptizing.

No sooner had I left the water and got on the grassy bank than the man we called the pastor had waded into the water with another man fully clothed. Quickly, the pastor immersed the other man. To the shock of everyone when the man came up out of the water, he began to shout loudly with his hands up in the air. I flew up the bank where my beloved Pap was. In a flash, I was under his arm asking in a desperate whisper, "Pap, what's happening to that man?" The wet man was now weeping and speaking in an unknown language. Pap's strong arm went around my young shoulders, and he spoke to me in his awesome wisdom.

"Daughter, everyone has the right to worship God any way he sees fit."

The sweet peace of God, which I have grown to treasure, settled over me. The man became quiet, and the small band of Christians who came with him helped him out of the water. They left without a word, but all had a smile of knowing on their faces it seemed. Pap's words have never left me and continue to guide me in the acceptance of people in their various forms of worship. I later learned the experience of that man was like those early Christians on the day of Pentecost and that same experience of being baptized in the Holy Spirit still happens today.

I know ... do you?

Used by Permission of the author JLM

I did not personally write this experience about such life down by a river, but I have heard the story over and over from the person whose story it is, and I never tire of its beauty and truths.

It is a multifaceted love story. The love of God who made an empowerment provision for His people from the beginning of the New Testament Church. The love of a grandfather, who shared time and self-frolicking in the water with grandchildren and who, at the same time, shared words of wisdom and offered a physical-emotional covering of protection to a young granddaughter who would one day testify to her own down-by-the-river experience.

Can we, as well, learn to let others go toward God at their own pace?

May we offer the same grace toward others as did this grandfather.

One Step Too Far

I will instruct you and teach you in the way which you should go; I will advise you with My eye upon you. Do not be like the horse or like the mule, which have no understanding, whose trappings include bit and bridle to hold them in check, otherwise they will not come near to you.
—Psalm 32:8-9 (NASB)

My phone blinking blue announced a new message was waiting: "Congratulations on your twenty-year anniversary of ordination." It was unexpected and disheartening. Unexpected because the date was unremembered and disheartening due to the timing. Yet, on the other hand, it was perfectly timed for a due path correction.

Let me explain. Despite the cries of my heart, the path of my walk as a servant has been littered with innumerable and varied types of *unintended* and every so often *willful intendeds* that range from simple unkindnesses with a slip of the tongue as well as some thoughts and actions that point to greater transgressions. This is a painful truth. Most recently, it is the *one step too far* that caused a due conviction to well up from within and has called me back again to my simple mantra and my foundational life objective of trust and obey.

Has God Said?

Has God said? Whose voice are you responding to? The call of a human or God? It matters, for one knows all things and the other simply some things. To follow the lesser voice, man's, may be infinitely more comfortable and expedient at times, but most often in the end, leads to an unfavorable finale. Indeed, one extra step in the natural can and has led some to walk off cliffs, into sink holes, and to be struck by vehicles. One step beyond instruction in the spirit has as much immeasurable negative potential: dim eyesight, dull hearing, and conceivably less than or no God usability. Sidelined.

Due Path Correction

Prior to going to a Christian gathering, the Holy Spirit quietly impressed upon my heart that there would be no fruit in responding to a particular request for prayer. Nevertheless, the voice of a godly ally prevailed over the still quiet one of God and the request was met. The time spent was pleasant, and in the natural, there was neither uncomfortableness nor any overt harmful consequences that I was aware of by my actions, and my ministerial friend seemed quite satisfied that I answered the prayer appeal.

And then, I went home to solitude to receive the correction. Once again, even after so many years of practicing hearing and obeying, I willingly took one step too far. God's instruction from the beginning was, "Do not pray, I'm not in it." Because the voice I followed was not His, there was no fruit from the prayer, in an otherwise attested to fruitful time of ministry. It was my offense, sin, transgression to own. With my confession of disobedience came peace, the lifting of my head and as always, a new day dawned with mercy.

We end where we began. God said through King David in Psalms, "I will instruct you and teach you in the way you should go; I will counsel you and watch over you. Do not be like the horse or mule, which have no understanding but must be controlled by bit and bridle, or they will not come to you." —Psalm 32:8-9 (NASB)

*God promises instruction. Instruction requires reception. The type of response to the reception equals the outcome. **Has God said?** Remember the little foxes... When you hear His voice do not do as I did at that time. Trust, obey, and **do not take one step too far**, for your life then will yield greater oneness with God, greater peace, and greater fruitfulness.*

Drink Deeply,
The Price of Wellness

*D*o *you want to be well?* This question was posed thousands of years ago by the great physician Himself, and it continues to call to all peoples today, for it is a non-gender, non-racial, non-socioeconomic, nor-age specific query. To all who have breath and ability, the call comes. *Do we want to be well in body, mind, and spirit?*

At first glimpse, some may disregard the question as irrelevant, or greater still, find it egregiously offensive. Why would anyone posit such a question? All want to be well. And yet is this truth?

What is wellness? Webster defines it simply as *the quality or state of being healthy in body and mind, especially as the result of deliberate effort.* A re-worded equation may establish well-being as a byproduct or side effect of a conscious and intentional endeavor. Therefore, if accepted, a relative state of health in body and mind seems attainable to those who have a capacity to think and act, if devoid of any grave pre-existing conditions in the mental or physical realms that would preclude them in the first place. If wellness, soundness, or stability is then within reach, why are so many not experiencing the gratification of such benefit in their lives?

The cost may hold the key. Self-ownership is a rite of passage granted to all persons legally, morally, spiritually when one comes of age. It is freely conferred. In contrast, *wellness* has a price tag marked *personal effort and exertion required*. To act, the status quo often must become so uncomfortable, so personally painful and unfulfilling that to move into the unknown future by taking full responsibility for self becomes a viable solution. For some, it may define as eating less, working smarter, playing more, changing friends, staying, leaving, losing status, being alone, or dreaming differently. No matter how it differentiates for individuals, the common underpinning is, *wellness demands action, and the cost of the action may seem too high a price.*

Consider, the well-being we address is not solely defined by lack of challenges in mind, body, spirit, but in the midst of them. Can any price be too much for one's wellness? This is an individual choice.

Today and into all our tomorrows when, not if, we hear the voice of our Creator asking, *do you want to be well,* I pray the courage for all to say yes. *Yes, I want to be well.* Yes, I want to drink deeply enough from the well of my salvation where healing was and continues to be provided.

Continually enabled and empowered by God's divine graces, through often costly personal choices, I elect and have elected to pay the price required for change to live out and sing, it is well with my body, well with my soul, well with my spirit, despite the assaults of living life on earth.

Drink Deeply

Boat Talkers, Water Walkers

Matthew 14:22-33

*D*arkness and mist played with pure sight. The sounds of the churning water in harmony with the whipped-up winds were thunderous and rocked the boat violently. Suddenly, a glimmer of a figure was spotted, and it seemed to be walking about in the storm on the water. Fear gripped the travelers' hearts. Was it a ghost? But with closer scrutiny there appeared a familiar figure to all.

One found his voice and called out, "If it is really you, Lord, as you just announced to us, bid me come." And Jesus said, "Come." With the formal invitation extended, Peter left the protection of the boat and the company of his fellow disciples and stepped out. He walked on the water until diverted, refocused by the reality of the raging natural circumstances about him, and then began sinking. With a cry of, "Save me, Lord," Peter then took the extended hand of Jesus and together they returned onto the boat. Instantly, the storm stopped raging. Awe and wonder once again pierced the small band of disciples in the boat that night as they trumpeted, "Truly you are God."

These same men, together with Peter, walked and talked daily with this God Jesus. They shared meals with Him, sat under His teachings on hillsides and in temples, walked on dusty roads, attended weddings, funerals, and other festivities of daily living. They had common friends, common enemies, and even common monetary resources between them. This band of disciples not only knew one another intimately, but they were recognized and known by government and religious rulers alike as followers of Jesus, the one who was defined as God by God through the attesting signs and wonders wrought at His hand and at His command.

Jesus called to all His that night, "Fear not, and take courage. It is me, Jesus." But only one responded back. Only one was called out. Only one went out. Yes, only one, although they were all in intimate relationship. The majority were stayed by their fears. They were immobilized. They would not break rank. They sat in their place of perceived safety in numbers. They looked in the natural and saw the impossible and doubted. But Peter trusted the voice and glimpse of the figure above the sights, sounds, doubts, and waited for the bidding. He went alone and faced the rage of the onslaught and was seemingly lost when he began to sink. But in his obedience and through his trust, Jesus was revealed that stormy night once again to His own people that He walked and talked with daily for years.

Peter's obedience qualified him. His natural fears did not overcome his spirit man. Fear did not prohibit him from bringing the glory and wonderment of God to others that night or across the annals of time. Peter, the water walker, was in the company of many safe boat talkers. Are we?

Today, God calls, "It is I." No matter how high the waves or black and gloomy the night may seem, He is present. If you hear His voice and see His figure, go as Peter. For safety, we have learned, is not automatically in numbers, nor in the familiar, whether boats, houses, paths, or relationships. True safety is where God calls each to. It is there that our disciple's walk, not our talk, will bring glory.

Call us out, Father, and grant us the willingness to walk not merely talk. And thank you that fear, stammering lips, and past failed attempts are not disqualifiers ...

Alignment

*M*isplaced something. Found it. Forgot something. Found it. Dropped something. Found it. The process repeated itself over and over and over again in such a short period of time that it was becoming mystifying as well as disturbing. Living in a rather small, orderly, and uncluttered environment, the possibility of the number of times the lose-find occurred would bend a statistical curve. Finally, the basic teaching with dawning arrived.

To be aligned in the natural is to be arranged in a position such as a straight line or in any other correct or appropriate relative position to other things. In astronomy, the things of the heavens are aligned, and in physical anatomy, the parts of our natural bodies are. In business, it is the linking of the organizational goals with the employee's personal goals. The church world aligns through doctrine, countries through agreement in treatise, mechanics through each part tooled and positioned to fit exactly to its corresponding part for functionality. Without correct positioning or alignment, a disorder, pain, conflict, ineffectualness, and even uselessness can result.

Although alignment or non-alignment, they have always had consequences, conceivably more relevant than in years past. With technology exploding exponentially, globalization is forcing alignment on the micro and macro scale for individuals, corporations, and nations. No life sector seems outside the circle. Positions are being taken consciously or unconsciously with impact.

This is the query: Are our present-day alignments God formed, for such a time as this? Philosophically, geographically, doctrinally, financially, relationally, are we in proper place? Are minor or major adjustments needed in order to know? Stillness and quietness are needed for correct diagnoses. Just as a mechanic listens to the sound of an engine, a doctor looks at and feels the body, weathermen gauge atmospheric pressures, business calculates numbers, and marriage counselors compatibility. Using our senses of touch, taste, sight, smell, and hearing in combination with personal knowledge, our answers will be revealed.

We must be able to perceive. Misplace something, find it. Drop something, find it. Forget something and find: *Alignment*. When we do see, find, realize, accept, will we embrace an adjustment, if prescribed. Choice is always present.

I end with a principle from the Word. "Do two people walk hand in hand if they aren't going to the same place?" —Amos 3:3 (The Message)

Think on the Power of Alignment

Two Roads

*W*hat road have you traveled down today? Can you remember last week's or even a month ago? For most, our destinations may be more easily remembered than the actual highways or byways traveled. These physical roads are just roads. They get us from one point to another with minimal thought in contrast to the issue or issues of life that put us on the road in the first place. Life issues have great inherent distinctions that command our attention. Some are voluntary and leisurely while others carry the weight and urgency of life and death. Each must discern.

In the New Testament writings, there is a man named Cleopas and another called Saul, both disciples who were traveling on different roads at different times with different purposes. Both journeys teach parallel lessons. Not unlike our early biblical counterparts, we are traveling a road in life. What can we glean from The Road to Emmaus and the Road to Damascus?

The beginning of discovery: The Road to Emmaus
—Luke 23:13-35

The Book of Luke records Cleopas and his unnamed friend as both being disciples of Jesus Christ. They were going about their daily business when one dramatic and disheartening event happened right on top another.

Word had just spread that Jesus, who had been crucified and buried a few days earlier, could not be found. The mammoth rock that sealed the tomb was moved, exposing the mysteriously empty burial place. The news brought with it another tsunami-like wave upon the Christian community. All were shocked, Cleopas and his friend alike.

And so, as they were walking the road this day toward Emmaus and discussing the alarming new information, a third person seamlessly joined in with them. Who he was they did not know. But the banter flowed between the two friends. How could the crucifixion have taken place and now His body be missing if Jesus was who He said he was? Who, really, was this Jesus whom they embraced as their King? Was He their Messiah, their God, as He had said? Were they led astray?

When the third person began asking His questions, they were in disbelief that anyone in the local area had not already been aware of the tragedies befalling the people of Jesus. The man took their rebuke in stride and continued to dialogue about the things of Jesus with them, explaining all that the scriptures had foretold.

As evening came and they arrived at the village of Emmaus, Cleopas and his friend asked the stranger to stay with them for a meal. He accepted, and it was only then, when He broke the bread and gave thanks, that their eyes were opened to see. It was Jesus, the One who had been sealed in the tomb days before, who had been walking with them all along the way.

Are we not often found to be just like Cleopas and his friend, who were so self-absorbed that day that they both missed the truth? The intensity of emotion and circumstance they were cloaked in clouded and overshadowed the voice of their inner man. It took a memorable symbol, the breaking of bread, to shake them awake. Too often it takes much, much more for us to awaken to truth as we travel on our ways …

Continuation of Discovery: The Damascus Road
Acts 9:1-9

On another day, time, and for a distinctly different purpose, Saul and his like-minded Jewish entourage were traveling on the road to Damascus hell bent on finding and bringing to swift punishment those who were followers of Jesus. Saul was consumed with his task of ridding the country of those who had the audacity to believe Jesus was the promised Messiah. His motto was death to one and all. And then suddenly a great light with a blinding intensity surrounded the group causing the leader, Saul, to fall to the ground. On hearing an unknown voice amid the chaos calling out his name he responded, "Who art thou, Lord? Jesus acknowledged Himself, but those with Saul were wordless. They heard noise as thunder yet saw no one and responded to no one.

With their assistance, Saul rose from the ground, with his natural eyes open, yet unable to see. Saul was blind. This proud, pompous man was now at the mercy of his undercharges who had to take him by the hand and guide him into Damascus. There a godly man by the name of Ananias was waiting to deliver a gift of divine intervention at the instruction of God. He was not pleased with the assignment. Who wants to be used to bless and deliver the enemy? Nevertheless, he was obedient and, as instructed, laid his hands on and prayed for the man who had tormented the early Christians who were known as the People of The Way. Miraculously, Saul's sight was restored, and it was the beginning of an exchanged life. This powerful, consequential encounter on the Road to Damascus with the Living God not only would transform his inner man, but God chose as well that Saul would become known as Paul, an Apostle of Christ.

Life, as we know, is seldom a straight line. As much as we would like it to be unsoiled and uncomplicated, it is not. Often, we tend to be like our brothers, Cleopas, Saul, and even the Israelites who predated them. They meandered around in the wilderness for forty years when an approximate eleven-day journey would have gotten them to their intended destination, if only they had had eyes to see, ears to hear, and hearts inclined to be obedient to what the Spirit of God was communicating.

What road do you travel on most frequently? Is it Emmaus where the circumstances in the natural obscure the truth of Jesus' presence in and with you day by day? Or Damascus, mirroring Saul's single-minded and relentless determination to do it his way. Or an Ananias, a servant-type who is fearful and grumbling, yet obedient, but would rather not be used in certain circumstances and with particular people? The overarching truth is that we have each most likely walked and continue to walk the way of the Emmaus and Damascus roads and presented as an Ananias at times.

A contemplation: Are we regularly, consciously, and actively in pursuit of receiving course corrections that will lead to piercing spiritual hearing, acute spiritual seeing, and commitments to using the gifts as God intends?

Let us go for our gold. We will find it along the way
as did Cleopas, Saul, and friends.

May we all be found walking on our assigned roads
in their due season.

We Are One

*T*his must be understood in the body of Christ. We are one. No one community church, house church, or mega congregation is an island to itself. We are one. No ministry or para church organization is an entity to itself. We are one. The truth of being one with the church in Asia, Africa, the Americas, Australia-Oceania, Europe, and every other local expression, the body of Christ, wherever it is found must be recognized and accepted by the people of God. As the Apostle Paul said, "We are one, with many members." When will we embrace this truth *in toto*? No part of the global body is more than or less than.

As a trumpet call, the sound must blow far, wide, and with clarity. Take down those dividing walls. This call from the lips of a former president was to a foreign nation years ago, but it was uttered in the heavenlies and heard through the voice of Jesus over 2,000 years ago. It was not directed to a single nation but to all nations, tribes, and tongues. *We must have ears to hear.* We must respond to the intent of our Father's heart. Jesus teaches oneness and unity in a spirit of love. This is the DNA of the true Christian. He tells us through the discourse with his disciple Philip that if you see and know me, Jesus, then you have seen the Father. This principle of truth holds true for all believers today. If we are in Christ, then others, when they turn their focus our way, should be glimpsing Jesus and His Father Who sent Him.

Unity In and By the Spirit

Are we that united? Do those around us intuitively know to whom we belong, or do they know us only by a stated affiliation? Does it really matter if we choose to associate within the framework of Catholicism or Protestantism if we have accepted Jesus Christ as our Lord and Savior? Does attendance at a Baptist house of worship cause offerings to be more acceptable to God than if attending a Presbyterian or Methodist church?

If found clapping hands and moving feet to the beat of drums in a non-denominational charismatic service, does that trump or negate the quiet, more meditative form of worship found within a Quaker gathering? If discovered worshipping on a Sabbath day of Saturday as Adventists do, does that make one less spiritual than most of the body that chooses Sunday? Tell me, is one less holy if they find life within a house church with few people instead of a cathedral with thousands? Is it acceptable to worship God on a Sunday morning from a mountain top, boat, or even a plane, instead of a pew?

I place these queries before all for consideration. Are these *the issues of our day* that the body of Christ and church leadership should be majoring in?

Can you hear the Lord imploring, be one and let me break down the dividing walls by allowing Me into the recesses of your hearts where doctrines and traditions of men have overshadowed *My Word*? Then and only then will the world see and know My love through you. They will see My Body loving one another as many members and many forms of expression as one united Body.

A change in one heart can be the beginning of a revolution.

But the hearts must be available …

Are Ours?

Is It Yours To Own?

*H*ave you heard the adage, "If the shoe fits, wear it," or as I often ask in pastoral counseling, is it yours to own? What are you embracing that is not yours to own?

There is an epidemic playing havoc with the souls of multitudes of people. Not unlike natural epidemics, this crosses every stratum known to man. If this affliction is your portion, then this is the moment in time to be extricated from the plague of it.

Would anyone you know deliberately purchase or take ownership of a pair of shoes that did not fit? The ramifications of wearing improperly fitted shoes are well documented by experts in podiatry. In layman's experience, shoes too big will cause tripping, too small, and the cramping of toes will sit you promptly down. If the heels are too high, in time your gait will be affected, and if too narrow or tight, bunions appear. Suffice it to say, if you own shoes that do not fit, you are in a place of distress, and change, without a doubt, is necessary.

The plague that many are now facing has to do with putting on, allowing, accepting, and receiving into themselves words, statements, and attributes ascribed by others, many times from loved ones, which are not truth. People are transferring and conferring onto those around them responsibility for actions and verbiage that has no truth in fact. *Perpetrators simply do not own their own behaviors nor the motivations for them.*

"It is your fault I hit you." "I would not have had to if you had been kinder." "My drinking is the direct result of your eccentricity." "If you would be more attentive to me, I would not need to spend so much money and time shopping." "You are always working; what did you expect me to do?" The litany can and does permeate throughout multifaceted relationships and issues.

The Costly Blame Game

If you are one of the multitudes who is being bound up unrighteously by the comments or behaviors of others, it is time to take inventory. Discard that which is not truth, and begin not accepting anything that is not truth, regardless of the source.

God said to bring everything into the light for the purpose of dispelling darkness. Our mental, physical, and spiritual well-being is at stake. Until we, or others, own our own issues of life, and not anyone else's, we will continue to be truncated in growth and our underdevelopment will eventually be a liability that may cost us in personal, family, and even business relationships.

Be extricated from the transferring of undeserved guilt and blame. We are called to walk in truth, not lies, deceptions, accusations, or innuendos. An opinion is an opinion, but not inevitably the truth unless God says it is so. Always test the spirit. God lives by and teaches that only the knowledge of the truth of any matter sets people free. When you embrace this principle and walk in it day by day, you will hear yourself saying...

"Free at last, free at last, thank God almighty I am indeed free at last."

Breathe.

In The Year King Uzziah Died

*T*he prophet Isaiah said, *"In the year of King Uzziah's death I saw the Lord sitting on a throne, lofty and exalted, with the train of His robe filling the temple."* —Isaiah 6:1 (NASB)

Is it not the cry of your heart to be able to say, as Isaiah did, "I saw the Lord. My eyes have seen the King. My eyes have seen the King, the Lord of hosts."

A few years ago, at a local Christian gathering, the following prophetic word was delivered.

"Isaiah said, 'In the year King Uzziah died, I saw the Lord seated on a throne, high and lifted up, and His train filled the temple.' I say to you this day that your God is a jealous God and will not share the throne of your heart with anything or anyone. In the year, *your King Uzziah dies,* you will see the Lord seated on a throne, high and lifted up, and His train will fill your temple."

The Word of God from the beginning of time through all of eternity will stand, will stand in toto. His commands and principles remain, and He is still sending his prophets to His people today declaring the will of His heart. Will we listen? Will we have ears to hear what the spirit continues to say? Will we receive it to ourselves and take it before the Lord and ask, "Is it I, Lord, you want to speak to today, concerning who is seated with you on the throne of my heart?" Will we allow the Holy Spirit free access to every person we are in relationship with, every financial decision we make, every social function we attend, every dream or determination we have from who we will marry, to where we will live, and to how and where we will utilize the giftings given to us in both the natural and spiritual realms?

Do we desire to see the Lord more than we want it our way? Can we believe that our gain, by having it His way, will be much grander than having it our way? Or will we stubbornly cling to and *be satisfied reigning with our little gods?*

This word is powerful and deserves due diligence for our intensive consideration. Is God calling through the Word and principle spoken so many years ago via the prophet Isaiah and restated again today through a willing vessel? Is it not the cry of your heart to be able to say, as Isaiah did: I saw the Lord, my eyes have seen the King. My eyes have seen the King, the Lord of Hosts.

Valley of Decision

An answer in the affirmative will cost you. The dethroning of anyone or anything will surely have an expense, but then Jesus said, "Pick up your cross, die to self, and come follow me." He did it Himself on Calvary for you and me. He chose the Father's will. Are we ready to do the same for Him?

Trust God for every grace needed as your heart is probed.

Plant, Nurture, Harvest

Keeping Right Perspective

*I*n life, all things have roles and purposes. Finding and walking in them is sometimes the challenge. When we seemingly find our places, we tend to grasp and hold onto them without factoring in the word *seasons*. For us to be out of step with the *season* or appointed period can carry consequences that range from the minuscule to the catastrophic. Compound the confusion of a designated role in each season and the multipliction of a negative happenstance has the capacity to increase exponentially.

Waltzing to disco music may look strange. Swimming in the winter may feel strange. A harpist trying to blow a trumpet may sound strange. Yet, being out of harmony in these instances may simply cause some laughter, embarrassment, and or some ridicule, but nothing that would rise to any great magnitude. On the other hand, if a five-year-old gets hold of a loaded gun or a fourteen-year-old begins driving down a major highway and a one-hundred-year-old is ordered into active military service, the ramifications to not only the individuals but those whose paths they might cross are greatly magnified.

Life in the natural requires knowing who we are, what we are called to do, and when. Identifying who, what, and when is mandatory for successful living. Am I the student or the teacher in this season of my life? Knowing matters. Am I the skilled surgeon or the patient in need of surgery? Role matters. Is the baby due today, tomorrow, or next week? Timing matters? Is it time to plant, and where do we plant these trees, grass, or apple seeds? Does harvest come in winter, spring, or fall for the individual various products? Seasons matter. What type of ground? Soil matters.

Life in the spirit mirrors natural life. It was designed that way. To be life producing in the spirit we need to know who, what, and when again. The Apostle Paul said some people will be called to plant seed, others will water the planted seed, and yet there will still be others who will be designated as harvesters of the finished product. It is not for the hand to do all, nor for the head to do all, nor for the feet to do all. It is for the head to get the feet and hands to the right place at the right time for their appointed task. Even as the whole body is needed to accomplish *the whole purpose, so is the right designation of each part in the appointed order or season.*

This is right perspective. This is natural and spiritual truth made simple. The who, what, when, and where of matters is not trivial. If you do not know what your role is or even what season you are in, it is time to ask God. Perhaps you are to be a student instead of the teacher. Time change. Are you the one in need of re-tooling for this present season? Have you simply tired of your post and taken leave, abandoning your assignment and leaving chaos in its wake? Or, are you the one sitting stoically when, in fact, great wisdom desires to course through you. You, unwittingly, are neglecting your calling and your purpose in this appointed season. The forward progress of others is being hindered because your voice of wisdom is not being released.

I pray we all hear the knock, where slumbering. God stands at the door. In the spirit, there is always a seeding, planting, watering, nurturing, and harvesting season in process. The body of Christ is needed, the whole body. Let us each be about our appointed assignments, for the time to know who, what, when, and where is now.

VI

CHALLENGES

VI

CHALLENGES

With breath comes challenge, and through the journey of life to our individual grand finale, challenge will be ever present.

Can we embrace challenge?

Carole's Story, You Hold the Key

*S*he was crying out: *"God, help me, help me"* when she saw a massive hand come down from above. He opened her prison door and bid her come out. Hesitantly, she walked out, but the sights and tastes, though not totally unfamiliar, were such that she retreated behind the closed door.

Again, she cried to God, "Please, help me." As before, the hand came and opened the door before her. This time she ventured out a little farther than at first. But the same feelings of uncomfortableness with the newness seemed to overpower her, and she quickly retreated behind the door. It closed her in as before.

For the third time, she beseeched heaven for help in her circumstances, and the hand opened again the door that restrained my friend. But she still could not accept the freedom, and for the fourth time, she found herself entreating God for the help she so desperately needed. This time, His response changed. The hand came down as before, but in it lay the keys. She heard His voice, with no condemnation, say, "When you are ready, you open the door, and then you lock it behind you. I will be here waiting, and then together we will walk through the changes to come. Trust me."

"God, help" is the most common refrain heard round the world. How many pleas to God, coupled with the seriousness of the issue and the intent of the caller, are known only by Him. And this is good and fitting. What a phenomenal, naturally incomprehensible truism! And it was the cry of God the Father's heart wanting relationship restored with His creation that set the stage for the cries of our hearts to be heard by Him. Because God so loved the world, those who call on His name not only have an eternal destiny with Him, they have a present-day destiny that includes having the Eternal God available to walk, talk, and take counsel with morning, noon, and night.

This same God who loves unconditionally is ever calling His people to growth and maturity. He came to set the captives free, and where His

Spirit is, there is liberty, sacred scripture says. But the price of liberty is to walk in it.

The cries of our hearts are heard from on high, yet God requires effort, obedience, and movement from His people. Israel had to move forward and walk out of Egypt (old ways of living life and thinking) toward the new or Promised Land. They had to do it. God would not do it for them. The way was provided if they would reach out by faith for the deposit of courage and trust needed. The prison doors of the mind are opened in the same way. Believing that God will meet you in every circumstance encourages hope. Hope leads one away from fear and limitations, and then the possibilities and potentialities without limit are attainable. It is trusting that something can and will change if a new action or reaction is brought to bear in the present-day circumstance or need.

What is it you need from the Lord today?

Your cries are being heard. You must believe that and believe God is waiting to walk you through into a new place where life will not feel, look, smell, or taste the same but will offer life in fuller dimensions.

Do not settle for the leeks and cucumbers of yesterday. God has so much more to offer, so much more. Take the key and lock your yesterdays up.

Turn: God is standing outside the door waiting to walk with you through the next one, as He was for my friend Carole.

Remember...

"You can do all things through Christ Who strengthens you."

This is truth.

The Lady By The Sea, A Divine Appointment

*S*everal years have moved by since encountering the lady by the sea, but the freedom that came forth for her on that day continues to echo through the chambers of my heart. Every time I am brought to remembrance of her, I am both humbled and awe inspired.

Scripture Declares the Mercies of God Are New Every Morning

At the age of ninety-three, as she stood on the sands gazing out at the sea near her home, the dawning of truth gently came upon her as she engaged carefully with this stranger. It was time to walk free of her past deeds and allow the shame and fears she had carried throughout her lifetime to be swallowed up in His love. It was time.

The lady by the sea was a Christian, a mother, and a friend to many. In the natural, she would have been considered quite successful, yet in the realm of the spirit, she had never experienced true peace. Why? It did not take long for the unfolding of her story, of sowing to her flesh. From early years and even into her later life, she had a sin that so easily beset her, as she so delicately put it as only a genteel woman would. She simply liked men, and they liked her as much.

In religious teaching and throughout her life, she was the woman at the well, but without the forgiveness and mercies of a loving God. She could not receive forgiveness *in toto* because it was never truly unconditional in her experience. She had not been taught that sanctification or cleansing was accomplished through and by and in God's power alone. She thought it was her sole responsibility to change herself. And because she had tried so many, many times to turn over a new leaf without success, she considered herself a stench and a wench in the sight of her God.

Where Truth and Mercy Meet

Her burdens were many, and the weight of her sin was even now very considerable at ninety-three years of age. Day in and day out, as she watched the ebb and flow of the waters, she longed for peace. As I stood with this lady by the sea, by divine appointment, the mercies of God which are new every morning were offered afresh to her. At last, she could hear and receive the rest of the Good News. She had been forgiven by her God, each and every time she confessed her transgression with a broken and contrite heart. Peace, the precious soothing sacred peace that eluded her all those years, was finally hers. She embraced truth. In her own sight, she was no longer an outcast to the God of her heart.

By now, My Lady is most probably in the arms of her true and eternal Lover, Jesus Christ. Yet, her story lives on. May we glean from it?

We must believe that no one and nothing is ever beyond the reach of His mercy until breath itself is extinguished by God.

Be on alert and aware for your next divine appointment. Someone's freedom may just be at stake.

The Pea Patch Assignment

*S*hammah was his name, and he was no ordinary man, for he was one of "David's mighty men," and to be one of the mighty was an honor. Most of the elite men slew many single-handedly and regularly defied the odds in battle as they maneuvered around and through the opposition with seeming ease. Yet, of all the mighty, Shammah alone held a singular distinction. He had the peculiarity of being given the Pea Patch Assignment.

Now after him was Shammah the son of Agee, a Hararite. And the Philistines were gathered into an army where there was a plot of land full of lentils, and the people fled from the Philistines. But he took his stand in the midst of the plot, defended it, and struck the Phillistines; and the Lord brought about a great victory. —2 Samuel 23:11-12 (NASB)

If we could choose how to go down in the annals of history, ponder how many of us would willingly be found in a lentil field defending it, when no other man, woman or child stood there nor was proprietorship or family ownership or economic advancement an issue. Why stand alone to do battle, putting one's life on the line to protect a simple pea patch, a lentil field that was nothing but ordinary? Why?

Yet, Shammah did just that. Once again, as is recorded, he took his stand in the field of lentils, defeated the Phillistines, and God brought about a great victory that day. *No more was written. It must be enough for gleaning ...*

Are we willing?

Can God count on you? Can He count on me? Are we willing to be found standing alone in nondescript places without fame or fortune? Are potential assignments, which seem at first glance too small, less worthy of consideration? Have age or preference of location become an influential factor? Have position, education, or title inwardly outdistanced or negated the would-be call? Or, on the other hand, have the ordinary positions of life filled you with such disdain that your patch of peas has long been wilted and your plot trampled with no detection of life whatsoever? Has slumber overtaken watchfulness and earnest stewardship bowed to slothfulness? Any strength left to stand? Do you even desire to stand in your place of assignment?

These queries and others like them need to be addressed if God is to have the opportunity to bring forth great victories in our day, whether we record them as ordinary or of monumental proportions. Shammah and the other mighty men all had one thing in common, regardless of their assignments. *They went, they stood where they were sent, and God's empowerments gave the victories.*

King Solomon with all his wisdom pondered the question, "Is there anything new under the sun?" The answer astoundingly and overwhelmingly is no. Seasons come, and seasons go. Assignments will continue to come, and assignments will go, but will we be found willing for the pea patch knowing ridicule, lack of understanding, and rejection may certainly be our portion?

See 1 Chronicles 11:10-14 for more on the Deeds of David's Mighty Men.

What is Your Isaac?

Genesis 22

*A*braham's story of old calls. Can you hear it? The familiar story goes that, at the age of one hundred, Abraham finally was in possession of his gift that God had promised to him and Sarah so many, many years before. The boy-gift was called Isaac, meaning *laughter*, and he was the delight of their old age.

A day of defining came once again to Abraham in an charge from His God. It was not the "leave your family and your homeland and come follow Me" that he heard as a young man, but rather, "Come, follow Me, and place your promised son Isaac upon My altar. I have need of him." Abraham, by the grace of God, was once again found obedient and completed his assignment of assignments. He dutifully took his son, tied him to the altar, and lifted his hand with a knife prepared to sacrifice "his Laughter." But the voice of instruction said, "Stop," and Abraham heeded it. Isaac's life was not required in the end that fateful day, only his father's obedience. The place was then called by Abraham, "the Lord will provide."

Do you have an Isaac in your life? Is there someone or something that lies deep within your heart that is so sacred, coveted, loved by you, that even God has no right to it, in your estimation? If so, the Abraham-Isaac story found in Genesis of the Old Testament will call you to look again at God's unwavering faithfulness to His promises made to His children, as well as His unending ways of teaching and providing for them when obedience has been evidenced.

Being a genuine follower of Jesus Christ requires more than mental and verbal assents. It requires aligning our behaviors with our verbiage, just as Abraham did through myriads of trials and testings. Time has not changed this basic tenet of the Christian faith, nor will it. In truth, our faith is known best when it is tried, and it is tried best when something or someone so cherished to our hearts is identified and called forth to be placed on the altar of God, by us. It is not an issue of if, but when a child of God's will be asked to place something on His Table. Are you prepared within to let go of that special someone or something at God's request as Abraham so dutifully did? Do you believe deep within your spirit that God will provide?

These questions need to be asked, and they deserve to be answered.

Probe diligently and honestly the depths of your being concerning a possible Isaac, but do it in and with the light given by the Holy Spirit.

Cry out for the needed strength to let go,
and trust that the Lord will provide,
even as He did for Abraham and all others in the Faith Hall of Fame.

Can you hear the old story of a father and his son?
If so, follow Abraham's example into obedience.
For it is in obedience that scripture says true favor is found.
Finally, remember, having an Isaac is not the sin,
but not being willing to release your heart's treasure is.

The Power of a Good Life

*Y*ears ago, the good works and compassionate service to the poorest of the poor catapulted a tiny-framed woman with a burdened heart and an ignoble spirit by the name of Agnes Gonxha Bojaxhiu into an international figure of monumental proportions. She reigned for years as the poster child of goodness around the globe. Princesses, presidents, and even movie stars flocked to be seen with the little woman who worked in the ghettoes.

These are the words of this woman who is better known as Mother Teresa of Calcutta. Hear them.

"There are many religions, and each one has its different ways of following God.

> I follow Christ:
> Jesus is my God,
> Jesus is my Spouse,
> Jesus is my Life,
> Jesus is my only Love,
> Jesus is my All in All,
> Jesus is my Everything.
> Because of this I am never afraid."

These are the words of Mother Teresa of Calcutta, again. Think about them more deeply.

> I follow Christ:
> Jesus is my God,
> Jesus is my Spouse,
> Jesus is my Life,

Jesus is my Only Love,
Jesus is my All in All,
Jesus is my Everything.
Because of this I am never afraid."

Multitudes were touched by her love when she walked this earth, and we can be assured the works of her hands are written forever in the hearts of the dying whom she ministered to in Jesus' name. And many, many can still be touched by the power of her life through her written testimony. Will you be one of those?

Read once again her explanation for her life, as it was lived. *The world embraced her and yet denied the foundation and power behind her life.* Yet, emphatically and unabashedly, this Nobel Peace Prize winner proclaimed and gave full recognition to her Lord and Savior.

Now you feel and know who the undeniable inspiration and foundation of her life was. Hear, know, and respond.

I follow Christ:
Jesus is my God,
Jesus is my Spouse,
Jesus is my Life,
Jesus is my only Love,
Jesus is my All in All,
Jesus is my Everything.
Because of this I am never afraid."

Will you say the same?

The same power that resurrected Jesus resides in us if we have answered His call. The same power that resided in Mother Teresa resides in all who have called on the name of Jesus. *That same power for living a worthwhile life is ours for the asking and taking.*

Mother Teresa was not born with a supernatural compassion, love, or the ability to touch the unclean that others would easily and readily pass by. It was worked in her by the power of the living God she said yes to.

We are no different than Agnes Gonxha Bojaxhiu, and she was no different than the characters found within the Word of God. Jesus said, "Come follow me" to Matthew, Mark, Luke, John, Paul, Abraham, David, Jeremiah, Deborah, Esther, Elizabeth, and Mary. We are no different than any of them. Each is given tasks in life that come with the options of choice. Those of old said yes, and Mother Teresa simply said yes to the One she called her "All in All."

Her modern-day yesses led to a power-filled life. Why not follow her lead?

Who doesn't want to be never afraid?

I give thanks for a modern-day figure worthy of emulation in word and deed.

No Room in The Inn

And she gave birth to her firstborn son; and she wrapped Him in cloths, and laid Him in a manger, because there was no room for them in the inn.
—Luke 2:7 (NASB)

Rejection

*R*ejection is a word, a concept, and a facet of life that most have experienced, yet no one desires. The extent and effect it will have will vary on those it touches and the circumstances surrounding it. For far too many people, rejection has or will be defining. Whether true or not, it will debilitate, truncate, twist, and stop life in some form. Yet, it need not. To be defined by our no's needs re-examination.

We can begin with the Christmas story. One starry night long ago, a life was about to be brought forth that would change the history of all ages, peoples, tribes, and tongues. At the due time, a notice of rejection was issued: *No room in the Inn.* And yet that *no* would not or could not stop what was to be. It simply changed the setting. Christ's public birth was followed by a life openly lived before all and ended just as visibly on a cross thirty-three years later, which mirrored the greeting of his birth and life on earth. No room. No place. No position. However, His life's rejections, hardships, sorrows were God's opportunities to lead Him to diverse peoples, in different localities, and into unusual circumstances that were necessary for the fulfillment of His purposes for all of eternity.

Believe

Will we believe? Can we believe that God continues to have purpose, all the way through every season of our lives, whether it seems as though we are living non-producing winters, nominal springs, oppressive summers, or extraordinary autumns? These no's are life's elements that attempt to define, defeat, and lead us into abysses where we self-identify as the no and where others speak about what has happened to us as though it is who we are. Could there possibly be greater purposes when doors close, positions are lost, relationships thin, loves dissolve, finances dwindle, and health declines than we are willing to believe for. Is loss never positive?

Look again at the manger, gaze at the cross. It is time to believe, to perceive our trials and tribulations as sifted through the hand of God are to position or reposition our lives to fulfill purposes that are yet to be revealed.

No room. No place. No position. The nos of yesterday and today hold the promise of tomorrow's yes. Remember, the No Room in The Inn declaration simply changed the setting of the event but did not and could not change the intended result. *Nos are directional, not fatal,* and every end will only make room for a new beginning. Will we believe?

I pray we are all given eyes to see the hope
on the horizon of each of our God-sifted no's.

Odd Man Out

*E*ver feel like the odd man out? No doubt some of us have experienced it more often than others, but it only takes one experience to belong to the Odd Man Out Club. Usually, the one experience defines our fragile senses. It is a most uncomfortable situation to be in. As Christians we enter this club automatically as we are transported from the world of the natural man and its corresponding spiritual darkness into the Kingdom of Light.

Whether at school, with friends, in the marketplace, or with family, do you find yourself, at times, stretching toward the things of the world because it is lonely at the water fountain, lunch table, or on Saturday nights?

In Proverbs 23:17 (AMPC), we are instructed, *"Let not your heart envy sinners, but continue in the reverent and worshipful fear of the Lord all the day long."* This sounds simple enough, yet it is not. If, however, we continue to verse 18, we find consolation, *"For surely there is a latter end [a future and a reward] ..."* That statement offers incentive and may lessen the very human natural inclination to lament about the things we cannot engage in and put in check any envy we may have toward those who can.

It takes courage to be numbered as the odd one out. *It takes discipline and internal fortitude* to stand against our own innate carnal ways as well as the ways of the world. Going with the flow is the prevailing mantra of our times, and it is recognized as the antithesis of God's direction. Which road shall one take is the query ever before us. Shall we fear our reputations at the hands of our culture, or shall we fear God's way?

It is a question worthy of consideration. It is a question we will always wrestle with. *"But we can do all things through Christ who strengthens us,"* the apostle Paul stated.

Wisdom says there is much more to fear than being in The Odd Man Out Club.

Construct, Deconstruct, Reconstruct:
The Actions of Life

*T*hese words are fascinating. The lessons to be found within the language, even more so. Think about life. Think about your life. Think about your life as though it is a house.

In the beginning, there was simply a thought, a plan, even a future plan, in someone's inner vision. The original design ideas were brought to the architect who systematically pulled together all the thoughts, making sure the design aligned with the prevailing housing codes. Finally, he or she put on paper the exact image or prototype of the dwelling, culminating in a master plan.

The diagram is then ready to be initialized, and the construction begins. But just before the house is about to be completed, circumstances arise that dictate a change to the original plan. Some of the dwelling must be deconstructed to make room for an unexpected but needed enlargement that was not part of the original plan. Reconstruction then follows the deconstruction phase of the original construction. Notice, the mandated changes to the master plan due to the changing circumstances did not require the house to be abolished entirely. The design simply needed amendment or adjustment for the accommodations.

Our lives, like this house, will go through phases. We dream a dream, and the blueprint is etched deeply within. We walk toward it, building through philosophy, education, relationships, positions, and spiritual inheritances staying ever close to our original prototype. Then unexpectedly, surprisingly unplanned life events happen upon us, some gently, some forcefully, and our original plan and some of its out-workings, some of its benefits, are deconstructed before our very eyes. In its wake, there is room for reconstruction. When the dust settles and sight is regained, a new plan emerges, even if ever so dimly at first. With it, the energy, the courage, the insight, all the tools needed to reconstruct become visible and within grasp if we are alert to them.

Choice then squares off with us and becomes ever personal all over again. Do we, will we, must we, how can we embrace this change that is asked of us personally, professionally, or in both realms? Are we able to entrust this house, our house, to take on a new form, a new dimension, without first envisioning for ourselves the final blueprint, the exact replica of the projected new life? In this process, in this inner journey, we will answer by default the query as to who or what we trust in?

The actions of life found amid the principles of construction, deconstruction, and reconstruction affect all of humanity. Nothing and no one escape change. Winds blow, rearranging landscapes; elements mutate according to temperatures and seasons, and the human body ages imperceptibly at times. Businesses downsize or expand depending on trends or forces. But again, nothing and no one escapes the necessity of change. *This is a truth that will work with us if we but choose to embrace it. Will we?*

Consider that the future speaks now: Take inventory and freely consent to the metamorphoses that await your life. Do not fear, know in whom you trust, and may your inner house in this season be filled anew with courage and expectation, for there remains a future and a hope where there is breath.

Peace Through Your Process

Praise Him in the Hallways

As my eyes go back and forth, I hear and see of excess, it seems from every corner of contemporary life. Excess baggage, excess commentary, excess gadgetry, excess weight. Larger, faster, and more. Can you hear the voices and see the strategies of contemporary commercialism at work behind the scenes? It seems at times that I am as a puppet in the hands of puppeteers, being directed to desire more increasingly, exponentially in everything natural. It is challenging. And it is on this point my wrestle commences.

Spiritually, my mind is running amok, questioning how extreme overabundance as a principle of God intersects with the excesses displayed on us and around us today versus the principle of moderation. Could the two coexist in peace? I have concluded they do, for there was an earthly king ages ago who showed and continues to show all people groups the way.

His name was Solomon, and his fame for wealth and wisdom was known by kings, queens, and/or commoners alike around the world. He was like a free-flowing river ever enriching people with that which was bestowed upon him by God. Never again would riches of this magnitude ever be entrusted to any other human being on earth. Why Solomon? Scripture records that he knew God as his "Source," and this pleased God. His confession anchored him amid extravagance upon extravagance, and wisdom upon wisdom. King Solomon's heart of humility was demonstrated by the manner of living his life. He lavishly, without apology, praised and honored His God in The Hallways of life … *And it is on this point that My wrestling ceases* … Solomon's story teaches that whether entrusted with little or much, neither is predisposed to be the people's enemy in the natural or in the spirit realm.

It is about attitude and gratitude of heart.
This truth is for the ages. It is not about what we have, but how we utilize it.
God, grant us the wisdom to know the difference.

Let us Praise Him in the Hallways of Life by The Actions of Our Living.

Anywhere but Nineveh

*Y*ou may have heard the story ...
One day long ago, God's word came to Jonah, Amittai's son: "Up on your feet and on your way to the big city of Nineveh! Preach to them. They're in a bad way, and I can't ignore it any longer." But Jonah got up and went the other direction to Tarshish, running away from God.
— Jonah 1-3 (MSG)

Being in lonely places, strange and unappreciated places, dry places, unexciting places, small places, too much or too little to do places, and every other uncomfortable place known to man will be our portion some time, perhaps many times in our lives. This is not new. But we must grasp the dire importance of knowing the measure of our faithfulness to the assignment is in direct correlation to the measure of our trusting in our God who is the assigner of assignments. Doubting, probing, and questioning the mission or placement are not problematic, but moving out and moving on without the Holy Spirit's direction is the indefensible. It is the stepping ahead or lagging behind the Spirit that causes unintended consequences for us that are often less than pleasant and may even exceed the original unpleasantness of the initial assignment.

Stepping out and vacating God's place for us is never a singular event, although it may appear that way with a cursory glance. Others we are in relationship with will be impacted as well, guaranteed.

Today, the Lord asks this question of you: "Why are you running from your God? And where do you expect to go that I cannot find you? It is I who caused you to be born, and it is I who has kept you these years. Turn back, come back now. To leave that which is familiar, that which I have entrusted to you, is not what I am asking of you in this season. I am asking you to stand."

Contemplate Jonah again. Like Jonah, who has not gone their own way at one time or another? Surrender to God your will in all the matters that have weighed you down and caused you to think that God is not with you in this anymore. You may be thinking it's time to move on because there is no life here. But God! It is stand or stay, not by feelings or by sight, but by the direction of the Holy Spirit.

The present call is for all to mature and stand or vacate according to God's will, depending upon what God is directing in your present circumstance. No more, no less.

VII

NATURE
Things Great and Small Teach

VII

NATURE
Things Great and Small Teach

*I*f we have eyes to see and ears to hear, no matter where we are or what we are doing, God seems to delight in opening teachings on life. The Natural world and the Animal Kingdom continue to be some of the most familiar arenas He uses to teach. Therefore, stay on the alert ...

Rocks Will Cry Out,
Grand Canyon 1

"I tell you, if these stop speaking, the stones will cry out!"
—Luke 19:40 (NASB)

*T*his was Jesus' response to the Pharisees who wanted him to mute the praises and adoration flowing from the lips of His disciples.

It is simply breathtakingly magnificent. Viewing pictures, listening to others' observations, flying over and around it in years gone by have never been adequately satisfying. Finally, standing on a precipice, overlooking the Grand Canyon, I was thoroughly touched by its grandeur. Every fiber of my being was at attention, although it seemed impossible to capture the magnitude of what my eyes were seeing. Visiting during the off-peak time of year made the experience so much more gratifying and infinitely more personal. It was as though an invitation had been issued and the tour was for two and no more: The King and me.

As I stood in awed silence, my heart was singing how beautiful is the universal body of Christ. It is deep, wide, colorful, and vast, not unlike the Grand Canyon. Simultaneously, this scripture rang through me, *"I tell you, if these* (my people) *become silent the stones will cry out."* The literalness of the statement by Jesus was magnified a hundred-fold that day. If God's children will not herald His majesty, He truly has made the firmament, the canyons, moon, stars, oceans, and birds, all of creation to declare His Glory.

The Grand Canyon indeed has a voice all its own for those who will listen in. I experienced it firsthand for myself that spring day. I have no choice but to echo what I heard with my eyes; yes, heard with my eyes. We must proclaim the praises and adorations due the King of all Creation. He is worthy. He is worthy.

Must the rocks cry out as our voices?
May it never be. May it never be.

The Squirrel, Grand Canyon 2

"Perspectives." Another Lesson from the Grand Canyon …

*A*s I stood on the ridge overlooking the Canyon, I heard a crunching sound nearby. Looking down and slightly to my left was a very ordinary North American gray squirrel scampering about, in and out and over the rocks near my feet. It was about its daily business, and my presence in no way seemed to be affecting his or her program.

The size, speed, and seeming carefree attitude of this squirrel as it navigated the ridge of rock and sparse vegetation was in vast contrast to my slow, methodical, and measured movements. From my perspective, it was a very, exceedingly long way down, and I did not want to get there from the top of the Canyon in any other fashion than by foot or mule transport.

If I could have had a conversation with the squirrel, I am sure from its perspective, my concerns of falling would have been considered in the realm of hysteria.

So, whose perspective is right; the squirrels or mine?

Does this question remind you of scenarios you may have had or presently are having in your own life? Perspective is really all about where you are, what you know, and where you have been. Have you heard the story of the elephant being brought into a room where all the people were blindfolded and then asked to identify what was brought before them? One touched the tail, another the trunk and another an ear. Each answer aligned according to their personal experience. Was one's perspective more valid than the others? The answer is no.

And so, it is with the squirrel and my perspective. Both were very legitimate assessments of the circumstances based on our individual data bases. The squirrel did not have to fear the heights or terrain because it was designed or equipped for just such a place. I, on the other hand, needed to exercise a prudent caution to account for my lack of agility and size. And so, it goes …

Can we agree that our perspectives and our relationships are so intricately intertwined that perspectives, not just ours, must be prayerfully considered before pronouncing judgment …

The Trail, Grand Canyon 3

Another thought from the Grand Canyon …

As we looked over the vast Canyon from the rim and then looked down, way, way down, one could glimpse an outline of what appeared to be a shelter. Sometime later, I came to know this was a resting lodge for those who trekked to the bottom of the canyon either on foot or by mule. By scale and from my perspective, it appeared to be no larger than a building represented in a miniature village or doll house. To the natural eye, it was minute.

Had there been more time I would have seized the opportunity to journey to the end of this natural wonder. But instead, I was left to my own imagination. I could see no reasonable way down from my vantage point, unless I had wings, of course.

The intrigue mounted, and I knew there were spiritual lessons wrapped in this splendor before me. What, Father, would be the measure of my understanding from this scenario?

Once again, the word *perspective* came to mind. The squirrels scampering on the rocks and the birds fluttering around near scrub trees would find a way down by their innate senses and giftings. Their paths down would differ as would most of the other varieties of wild inhabitants of the canyon. This is not to say there would not be similar or even perhaps some crossover routings, but all in all, each would find their own way. And naturally, the pathway down for people would differ as well.

We can easily and readily grasp this truth of varieties of ways for varieties of species. Different trails, methods, or modes are natural until we begin poking around in the things of the Kingdom of God. Often, reason takes flight, and truth is lost. We bury uniqueness and call all of humanity, whether family, friends, coworkers, denominations, forms of governments etc., to a like and similar path to ours. We forget God made people in *His* image, not ours, and in that, scripture declares creation to be fully His expression. Variety does seem to be God's way, as evidenced by all of nature.

Are you struggling with the route people around you may be taking in choices and decisions they are making? Is frustration mounting because one you love is not following your prescribed path? Do you believe they have stepped too far off the trail you are familiar with, and they are forever going to be lost and unlocatable? Are you fearful for your own future or your children's because you cannot see tomorrow's way? Money may be scant, your marriage may be on the rocks, or your health may be less than beneficial. The voice of reason is screaming there is no way. And yet, there is a faint ol' familiar sound. It says, "Have Faith. I Am the Way.

Be encouraged. The trail has already been forged by the Trail Master. The way around, down, up, or over has already been mapped. Your personal Grand Canyon has a trail, and you have been perfectly equipped for the journey. You must see it in the spirit, as it is too minute, yet grand, to see by the natural eye. He made it that way.

The trail is there. God says so. Shall the clay argue with the potter?

But remember always: *Your trail is unique.* He has many ways for others to find Jesus, just as assuredly as you did.

Entrust those in your heart and their trail to God! He is able.

The I Am and The Ladybugs

One day, I was dozing on my bed when my attention was captured by a small but persistent movement on my ceiling. Once focused, I realized I was looking at a ladybug that was on a journey across the ceiling toward the opposite side of the room. With a little more investigating, I spotted the reason, another ladybug. Whatever their relationship was, the bug overhead was on its way toward the other at the opposite side of the room. Its physical size, in comparison to the mass of ceiling to be navigated would make for a mighty long undertaking, one step at a time, I thought. Step by step, this little creature did, however, have a predetermined destination.

I was fascinated by the minuteness of the Lady as though I had never really seen one before. Intrigued I continued to watch her progression, first pondering her ability to make the journey, and then wondering if the timeline would be so extended that slumber would overtake me. But just as I was contemplating this, to my utter surprise, out came her wings.

My God-lesson became absolutely clear on the issue of equipping. How often do we assume and prejudge our circumstances with such thoughts as: I cannot, it will not work, I do not have, or I am not able? The journey forward seems so far away and next to impossible. Time, finances, health, skills, or giftings seem too minimal for the task, not unlike the initial thoughts concerning my Lady Bug before I was startled by the unfolding of her wings.

But... but... but...

As maturing people, our *buts* are and must be countered by the Word of God. In Philippians, it is written, *we are able*. Ephesians explains the why. We are God's handiwork, His workmanship; therefore, I am. Scripture records in Philippians that I am amply supplied, and the proclamation that we are equipped is found in 2 Timothy.

We are equipped, able, and amply supplied for our life journeys just because we are His. I am, you are, just as the Ladybug. *We must not get confused or downcast by what we see at first glance or how we feel.* Like the Ladybug, when it was time to make haste, after many small steps, the *empowerments*, the wings that were hidden, came forth to take it to its destination. What seemed an improbable or impossible mission was not.

Make a conscious choice today to believe that the Great I AM of Moses' day is still sending His people forth, and that I AM has sent you and me. Not only has He sent us, He has additionally equipped us.

*I pray we will be granted eyes to see
when we think something is impossible.*

Her Name Is Precious

*A*nd God said, "Let the earth bring forth every kind of animal—
cattle and reptiles and wildlife of every kind." And so it was.
—Genesis 1:24 (TLB)

After making His creation, God always ended with the commentary,
"... and it was good."

A litter of seven Airedale pups were born, four males and three
females. The males found families immediately, so when I arrived on the
scene, three females were presented to choose from. As I stood and
watched the dynamics of their play, it did not take long to ascertain the
one who was neither the largest nor the smallest nor was she highly
thought of. In cycles of minutes, she was routinely either ignored or
cruelly pounced on by her siblings. Her tail tucked and her head hung
low, she simply cowered at my approach.

Wise people know this is not a good sign, but I followed my heart,
paid the fee for her freedom, and took the shivering little fuzz ball home.

An eight-year journey began...

And her name shall be *Precious*. When the name was presented to
me by a friend, I thought, *No, too clichéd for my tastes.* However, instantly
within me, I heard, "Her name shall be Precious." The name was as settled
as John the Baptist's so many years before. The naming seemed over used,
but it would stand. Only with the passage of time would I come to understand her name would correctly prophesy who or what she would become
under a banner of love. Yes, it was a good measure of time through multitudes of experiences and adventures of life together until, at last, she exhibited all the classic traits of the stately Airedale Terrier. Noted for their
loyalty, intelligence, trainability, and non-obtrusive ways in the home, she
became all of this and more. Precious has moved on now, but the lessons
taught through her continue.

There is hope for you, and for me. He is called The Banner of Love.

Certainly, some of us resembled the pup Precious in dimensions of our lives at some point in time. Perhaps fearfulness, awkwardness, or physical simplicity overshadowed the essence of one's identity. An adverse touch of a cruelty, an unfairness, a prejudice, or a coveted relationship that was broken may have caused a response to cower, tuck tail, and hang the head low.

Seasons of life have gone by since the flavorings of these happenstances: What do we mirror now? I hear the call to go back to Genesis, back to the beginning. It was there that His banner of love came over us. It was there that He proclaimed the raw material of His was good. We must believe it, for He said it was so. The blood of Jesus poured out on the Cross sealed the Love.

Who are we to argue with the Potter?

Ponder this truth. We are *becoming*, just as Precious became *precious* in time under the banner of human love. Refrain from self-judgment and self-loathing. Come out from under the heavy, deadly hand of condemnation from others and self. Give God time and room to work His wonders.

We too are precious and are becoming,
becoming under the hand of Love Himself.

Go prophesy, speak it forth … I am good. Self Esteem, Rise.

At the Scent and Senses

*D*ogs. I love dogs. The lessons of life have been many that I have received by the instruction of canines. This is simply another. Consider it.

Sight or scent, which motivates? This depends on the breed of the animal, as all are not alike. The predominant characteristic or sense of a sight animal dictates its modus operandi as does the sense of smell in another. A Greyhound activates its chase at the sight of its prey, and a Basset Hound by breed has its nose to the ground ferreting out its object of desire by sense of smell. Neither is better than the other, although we know within breeds, like people, some will excel. Predetermined giftings take cultivation, then opportunity to hone, develop, and mature.

As well, the five senses of hearing, taste, touch, sight, and smell that are gifted to mankind for the exploring of life ebb and flow in all, with varying degrees of predominance. Some are predisposed to hearing sounds or pitches that others cannot, while the taste buds of yet others can identify even the most minute dash of an ingredient within a food. Science has discovered scent to be intermingled in mating choices within the animal and human kingdoms alike.

The Word of God speaks to scent and senses as well. *"For a tree, there is always hope. Chop it down, and it still has a chance—its roots can put out fresh sprouts. Even if its roots are old and gnarled, its stump long dormant, At the first whiff of water, it comes to life, buds, and grows like a sapling* (Job 14 MSG). *"But solid food is for the mature, who because of practice have their senses trained to distinguish between good and evil"* (Hebrew 5:14 NASB).

Teachings abounded in my early spiritual development that decried the usage of natural senses as though once the things of God became alive, all else was to be muted. And yet this could not be farther from the truth, not then nor now.

We are called to exercise all of what we have been given in the natural and spiritual dimensions. 1 Corinthians 15:45 (NASB): *"So also it is* written: *"The first man, Adam, became a living person." The last Adam was a life-giving spirit.* As Christians, we know the last Adam was Jesus. Comparing differing bodies is of no avail. Both are necessary. The Apostle Paul exhorts in 1 Corinthians 15:40, *"There are also heavenly bodies and earthly bodies, but the glory of the heavenly is one, and the glory of the earthly is another."* The sun holds one glory, and the moon and stars, likewise, have their own.

Therefore, all have a glory. Maturity calls for unity of purpose: body, mind, and spirit. It is for each segment to be exercised and trained to their highest for their intended glories. While on earth, can the spirit say it has no use of its containing body? Can the body say it has no use of its spirit, which instructs in other realms? The answer is no.

Together let us celebrate our unique scents and senses,
giftings and aptitudes, remembering life's prototype is
both natural and spiritual. Let us be found exercising fully,
both our natural and spiritual bodies for the glory of God.

Dogs, More on Dogs

Bubber

*M*any years ago, I came across the following six lines on a calendar, and they still instruct me today. I call that a living lesson and savor the moment I stumbled across the month featuring *Bubber,* although the author was unknown.

I confess again, unashamedly, to being a lover of dogs. Most days, it does not matter what coloring, size, or shape these four-legged creatures are featured in. I seem never to tire of the thrill of watching them in action and, on occasion, wonder if I could be using my time more wisely.

Nevertheless, the story on the calendar went like this: "I had a big dog named Bubber who was one of my most important teachers. He used to sit out on our deck up in the mountains and just look. It was difficult for me to imagine what he was looking at all the time. So one day I went out and sat beside him, and for a long time, experienced just sitting and just looking. One sees so much when one just sits and looks. Bubber has since died, but his great wisdom in having taught me to sit and look lives on."

No doubt about it. God's thumb print is vivid on all of creation, if we will take time to see.

Airedale Tiara

Now to Tiara, who at first carried the name "Tara" by her birth owners. *Earth* was the meaning of her name, but it did not seem to fit, at least then. She was a dog in need of rescue from a pack of Airedales bred to hunt. She was small and gun shy. In fact, she was fearfully terrified of most sounds, whether a book dropping indoors or the rustling and crunching of fall leaves underfoot. She was a tried-and-true reject for the purposes for which she was bred. Tara, or Earth, was not wanted any longer.

If I secretly entertained the idea that I had learned all of my needed lessons through my Airedale named Precious and the unknown Bubber, I was delightfully mistaken. God's signature was as powerful and undeniable on Tiara, whom we called "T" for short.

As T grew older, and we had walked together for several years, it seemed a phenomenon was becoming more defined. Her terrier nature seemed to be accentuated. This is a very polite way of saying that, from time to time, her self-determination, head-strong, self-will had led her astray and into perilous situations. It had been as though I was staring at myself in the mirror. It was horrifyingly unsettling and gave new meaning to the Word of God that tells us that God's mercies are new every morning, and His compassions will never fail (Lamentations 3).

God knew all along it would take a few years until I could see in greater depth the meaning of T's name change. Not unlike T, we, too, have been formed from the earth, or flesh if you will, and with God's divine interventions we, too, are becoming like a Tiara, or a crown in His hands. Becoming is our journey. It is not too different from that of Bubber, or Precious, or …

I know from living with Tiara that there is stubbornness and self-determination that must be transformed in me, with numerous other notable characteristics, before I am crowned. But there is hope.

What traits might you exhibit that are, well, canine-like
that God is waiting to transform?
May God bless our honest assessments.

Unexpected Packaging

A call came unexpectedly from an unexpected source. The message left on voicemail was in the form of a question: Would I consider *re-homing* an elderly person's dog, and if so to please call the number as soon as possible for more information. Then the addendum, "Of course, there is no pressure to do this."

Intrigued, I soon made initial contact with the elderly woman armed with a slew of questions pertaining to her desire to find a new home for her beloved pet Happy, or more formally known as Mr. Happy. My intrigue rapidly morphed as Happy was described as a light brown, eight-year-old male miniature poodle who weighed in at eight pounds. His dimensions sounded more cat-like than my concept of a dog. But after considering the breed and size for a few days, to my own great surprise, I phoned and made an appointment to go and meet both owner and dog in their environment. The time spent was pleasant, but I left as I came, alone, stating I needed more time to contemplate the entirety of the situation.

After a few more days of wondering and talking to God about the variety of potential issues involved, I walked out of my comfort zone and loaded up Mr. Happy with all of his earthly possessions, with a caveat. For this to work, he would have to blend into a home that had another dog who visited daily at free will. They had to peacefully co-exist for permanence. All parties agreed. Within a few days, it became quite evident that Mr. Happy and Miss Scarlet were not a match from heaven, although age and size were. They just could not co-exist serenely. The snarky interactions exhibited by both canines portended trouble, and therefore, Mr. Happy could not remain with me. I was keenly aware that if I acted solely on my long-awaited self-interest to have another pet, one or both animals would undoubtedly experience harm.

Questions formed immediately. Why the unexpected call from the unexpected source in an unexpected package of a dog? *Was God calling?* What teachings required learning or re-learning through this small and insignificant matter in life? But then on further reflection, the words alertness, awareness, and willingness re-surfaced.

Attentiveness, alertness, or vigilance are precursors. When we ask God for an answer to a cry of our heart, we must be found awake, not slumbering, believing, not unbelieving, ready to hear or see, not unlike a sentry posted at the gate of a castle, or as a watchman on the wall of a fortified city. There must be a heightened consciousness of the circumstances and of those about us. We should be in a full sensory state of preparedness. But then, are we willing? Are we willing to consider, to receive God-answered prayers that present *differently* from our pre-existing mindsets of how it will feel, look, smell, sound, or taste?

All eight pounds of Mr. Happy were just such an example for me to ponder. Although he was found not to be the answer to my prayer, he was without a shadow of doubt one small package used as a mighty instrument in the hand of God to remind me again that His ways and His answers to prayers *are not limited to or by individual human preconceptions.*

This I know: He calls me afresh to be on alert, to be aware, for His answers to prayers are coming. They may, however, just be packaged in unexpected ways. He asks, will you be willing to receive them?

VIII

A TAPESTRY
Character Formation

VIII

A TAPESTRY

Character Formation

ife in the Spirit.

Multidimensional.

Lively Adventures.

A Note on Dandelions

*S*ome time ago, I was given a gift. On opening the small package, I found a note titled *The Parable of the Dandelions.* Underneath the note, at the bottom of the box, sitting on a liner of cotton was a multitude of tiny dried dandelion seeds. My first thought, without context, was *how odd a gift* followed by the discovery of how inordinately fragile the fluffy seeds were. I decided it was time to read the note.

This is what was written: *"As I was taking a walk, I noticed dandelions dotting people's yards. I was caught up in the wonder of these little seed pods. As I reflected on the incredible mind that designed this method of procreation, sending seeds on these fluffy wings of dandelions, it hit me how ironic this is. Wings and flight bring images of life and being upward bound. But seeds are made for dying, for before life comes forth, they must die. The flying and dying of these seeds are a refreshing picture to me of my life in Christ. Dying, yes, but on wings of a dove."*

In my acquaintance's extremely diminutive scroll, she said, *"Here are some winged seeds that you can do with as you like. Perhaps send them on their way, even as you continue your own journey."*

That is exactly what I have done, after finding the gift tucked away for over ten years. I released seeds of dire need for my own life. Given flight as the wind took them away from me, I asked God for new life, new *fruit* to come forth in the form of *love, joy, peace, patience, kindness, goodness, faithfulness, gentleness, and self-control.* These are the very character attributes He died for in lieu of the overabundance of weeds in the garden of my fleshly heart, which had been silently at work choking out greater life in the spirit. Dying to my natural inclinations of vocalizing and acting out over unlikeable circumstances without checks and balances or self-discipline is a *daily act of submission to the heart of God* that will bear the fruit the world is looking for. God said His people would be known by *fruit*, not spiritual giftings or theological pontifications, nor a legalistic adherence to the Word of God.

Regarding time, it is in God's hands. If this is true, the dandelion seed pods were rediscovered in a *due* moment. Prepared and waiting for me, dormant for over ten years, they, in their death, would still yield results, whether their reproduction season for their species in the natural had run out or not. Life in the Spirit has no expiration time frames, and its fruit is ever ripening.

The Book of Galatians calls death the way to greater life, as the *Dandelion Note* exhibits.

Hurl your seed pods upward, ask for the maturing that is needful, and wait for the return of new life. The world is watching with you …

As always, may our lives be more God honoring in and out of season.

The Wannabes vs. The I Am

*W*hat camp are you in? Are you a Wannabe or an I Am? Take time and consider the question. It just may cause you an awakening. What is a Wannabe? Wannabes are just that ... They want to be what they are not.

Brunettes want to be blondes, and blondes now want to be brunettes.

Ultra-thin people wannabe a little more chiseled, and those tipping the scales in the other direction wannabe a little thinner. Some married people wannabe single again, and some singles are salivating to be wedded. There are senior citizens who wannabe teens and teens that wannabe ... well, older.

The Church Wannabe

The pastor wants to be on the foreign field, and the missionary wants to be in the home field.

The worship leader wants to be the pastor, the evangelist wants to be a counselor, a teacher wants to administrate the church funds, and the secretary just wants to be appreciated. So, it goes.

There are multitudes, throngs of wannabes, and, in fact, most are afflicted by this terribly unhealthy syndrome at some point in time. We wannabe what we are not and want what others have. We just want and wannabe ...

On the other hand, we also have the I Am.

They seem to know who they are. They are not defined by their material possessions, their physical attributes, nor who they know or other common societal standards. They reside in a place of self-acceptance and contentment that pays rich dividends. The principles that guide them are simply biblical—thou shall not covet, contentment is godly, and love your neighbor as yourself, to name just a few. I could further speak of the attributes of the I Ams, but I know that you know when you are in their presence.

Where do you reside much of your time? Camp Wannabe or Camp I Am? Time for a change? The price and the way have been paid in advance for well-being. Shed the grasping within Camp Wannabe. Camp I Am awaits. Guaranteed, it will take a bit of energy to enter, but the investment to exchange camps will pay big dividends, such as … Peace.

Jesus knew Who He was.
So should we.
It is imperative.

Psalm 23

*T*his was King David's confession concerning who his Shepherd-Lord was. Is it yours? Let us look once again at this beloved Psalm, for it is now where we have need of David's Shepherd. It is in this moment of time where God's disciples are tested, challenged, and engaged on the stage of life for all to witness. It is always in the present of today when we hear the voice of God as a Shepherd calling that we are brought to a holy place of decision.

Personal comments or working definitions are in Parentheses.

The Lord is my shepherd
    (a deliberate, decisive, definitive association is made)
I shall not want
    (an emphatic declaration with no quantitative measures implied)
He makes me lie down in green pastures
    (guided gently into life producing lands)
He leads me beside still waters
    (waters that are gentle and bring rest into being)
He restores my soul
    (reestablishes, replaces, makes right the wrongs within my being)
He guides me in paths of righteousness for His name's sake
    (correct position that is unearned... in Him.)
Even though I walk through the valley of the shadow of death
    (deep darkness, trials, and tribulations- here and now on earth)
I fear no evil *(harm)* for God *(my shepherd)* is with me.
Thy rod *(of correction)* and thy staff *(of authority)*
    they comfort me *(settle, not threaten or coerce me)*
He *(God Himself, neither a stranger nor one who has been employed for the purpose)*
prepares a table *(life)* before me in the presence of my enemies
(unbelievers as well as others who want to do harm, not help)

God *(Himself)* anoints my head with oil
> *(His supreme mark of ownership and thus He takes responsibility for me and you, if you choose Him)*

My cup *(my life)* overflows
Goodness and loving kindness *(sweet mercies of inspiration)* will follow me all the days of my life *(on earth as it is in heaven)*.

He is your personal Shepherd, or He is not and or He has been. Whatever your position, let heaven know anew your answer today. Come.

Psalm 23 can be your path to peace in life on earth.

Jesus, the Good Shepherd of John 10
Jesus, the Great Shepherd of Hebrews 13
Jesus, the Chief Shepherd of 1 Peter 5

A PRAYER

Father, today, I renew my decision to have Jesus be my Shepherd, to be my Lord, to be my Commander In Chief. I cast off me, my yesterdays, and cast from me those people and circumstances that have led me into what they have wanted or wanted me to be.

Father, today, I align my thoughts with your truth that I shall not want, nor lack for any good thing and that you will always be faithful and true to me because that is Who and What You are. You will not leave me nor forsake me, as Your Word states, and that I have exactly what is needful for today. I choose to give thanks for my daily bread in food, strength, and monetary resources. I thank You for the clothes on my back and the roof over my head, just as they are. Father, forgive me for not trusting You. Forgive me, Lord, for doubting, murmuring, and complaining about my circumstances, of which You are aware. I pronounce as King David, *I shall not want.*

Father, today, I affirm Your ability to give me green, fresh, verdant places in You. I thank You for new depths in Your Spirit, new knowledge, new equipping, for my natural and spirit lives.

Father, today, lead me into waters of rest, that place where I may fully lean on You and not look at my circumstances or let the words of others cause me to react or implement any plan contrary to Your will and choosing for me.

Father, today, I am ready for You to bring restoration. Take my inner brokenness, my disappointments, my hardships, and my dreams of yesteryear into Your hands and transform them into a thing of beauty. Father, I am ready to give up my attitudes of slothfulness and neglect of You and all matters relating to Kingdom living. I am ready for You to bring a refreshing, a freshness to all my relationships, primary and secondary. Return to me the delight of the Lord, and restore my strength. Pour Your Spirit upon me once again, as I minister in the House of my God. Remove the hardness from my heart in all arenas of my life.

Father God, re-establish me. I give thanks that restoration is Your godly business, and You excel above all others in it. Thank You for showing me the way.

Today, I renew and rededicate my life as David did. Today, I freely choose and do proclaim Jesus as my Shepherd. Today, I bookmark a YES for new beginnings, knowing I can count on You.

Gratefully and Humbly,

Just Me

Tensions

*F*or most of us, there are enough tensions built into our everyday lives that if someone asked us if we wanted to contemplate those tensions within Christianity, most would say, *No, thank you. I will leave that to the scholars, philosophers, and ministers of our age.* Yet, to be a follower of Jesus, we often must do just the very thing we would rather not.

As Christians, we must face, and not fear, the tensions within our faith. Jesus describes in Colossians 1:15 the image of the invisible God who is also the First Born of creation. Plainly, this scripture says if we want to know more about God and what He is like, we need to look at the life of Jesus. As we examine His life, initially it seems exciting. We see Him healing the sick, befriending the notorious, and thumbing his nose at the legalistic religious figures of His day. Some would say this God is worthy to emulate.

Yet, fast forward this God life a few years and find Him hanging naked and beaten on a cross crying out for His Father, *"Eli Eli, lama Sabachthani,"* which translates, *"My God, my God, why have You forsaken Me,"* and our perception changes. The instruction to look at Jesus as the mirror image of God, and then to see Jesus in great unspeakable anguish, seemingly left alone by His God just at the point of greatest need, is a sight/taste of abandonment that is both bitter and chilling. No matter how we want to paint the picture, it seems as though we have aligned ourselves with a loser God who will tragically leave us when we most need Him. This is extreme tension and a necessary point to ponder. When God leaves you hanging on a life cross in your circumstances *with no felt consolations, no seen changes, no sense of hope, no articulated answers, or a directional plan to implement, and you inwardly experience jeering voices proclaiming you to be a loser, as Jesus and His Father, will you run and hide from your accusers or embrace the tensions found within your faith?* I pray the latter.

Faith tensions and crises will always present. The strength to stand firm and make peace with the tensions that wage war with our minds, wills, and emotions day by day is available. Look at the cross that seemed to defeat. Hear the words spoken, *"It is finished."* Go to the tomb that was found empty. Feel the emerging strength from within once more, respond to *He is risen* and seated, and *all things are in subjection to Him.*

Defeat is an illusion and not to be feared.

Today, may we see as God sees our tensions.

Moving on Again, Again, and Again
Such is Life in the Spirit

*A*nother assignment was coming to completion. I found myself pondering if God was the instigator behind the beginning dribbles of my discontent. Out of nowhere dissonance within came more frequently to the fore. Quietly, it approached until one day I sensed the writing was on the wall. Then, over and over, I repeated to myself, *the writing is on the wall; the writing is on the wall*, but the meaning was not yet known. However, within weeks, information came to light that would trigger the courage to believe it was God saying, "Stay, do not move into the new territory yet as planned. Stay." And so, without full understanding, I stayed, saying no to something I thought was mine, as well as my place to be. After the articulation of no, came peace, and weeks after the peace, came the awaited release.

Moving on … again. With this startling release from the year-long now *old* assignment came thoughts of new possibilities and vistas. The nature of this *new* work, if the door opened, had never before been considered by me. It simply seemed illogical from a natural point of view. The stages of unveiling were unwrapping slowly. The path lacked true clarity, and the reasoning behind all the change was still to be known, but *the peace* that passes all understanding *was now in residence*.

Obedience to God's ways is neither for the traveler who has predetermined their own journey-agenda nor for the weak in heart who must dare to stay or go. With stammering lips and trembling knees, assent is given, but unbelief and doubt have no weighted place for those seeking God's Spirit direction. *Trust does not demand sight. It simply believes.*

I began walking again and going someplace new to do something different. I could not tell you all the particulars because they had not yet been revealed. How long? How much? Why or When?

Yes, I, too, would have liked to know much more of the details beforehand. But it was not God's blueprint to unfold all at that moment in time. The plan would complete with each "yes" walked out.

One day someone said to me, "Your yes to God was why we met." I thought for a moment and responded back, "But it took your yes, too."

Will you travel, on your own journey, to that place of willingness?

Life awaits.

My Grace Is Sufficient for You ...

*G*old and silver are some of the most precious natural commodities known to man. Throughout scripture, our characters are likened to these commodities. It is God's intention to refine His children, and this process or business of the Holy Spirit is no different than that of a master crafts-person whose intent is to create the most magnificent piece out of the yet to be fashioned material before them. The instruments used to transform the raw materials are determined by the masters solely. They predetermine what is necessary, when it is required, and how much is essential to accomplishing that which is either on paper or in their mind's eye.

Simple enough, we may say, until ...

In the realm of humanity, elements such as pride, selfishness, and su-periority often say, *I am not broken; it is those others that need the adjust-ments.* Have you ever attended a service and thought, *Lord, I have no need of this message? It is my spouse, friend, brother that needs this correction or admonishment?* Have you ever sought counsel but inwardly reasoned that the wrong person was being counseled? Or, have you ever experienced a discipline at work while thinking *wrong person* again?

Then off one goes with a self-renewed sense of innocence to overtly share with the others how they missed their life-changing message or challenge.

A Call for Receiving God's Grace

Instead of actively engaging in transference, we must diligently pursue truth and allow the workings of the Great Potter to fashion us according to His ways. The attitudinal adjustment theory, *for others only,* is *denying our own humanity* and binds up the tool offered by the compassionate Master Craftsman for His subject matter at hand. That tool is *grace.* When God told the Apostle Paul that His grace was sufficient for him in his circumstances, He was presenting a principle for all through the ages, and let us not confine the graces given to one type of malady. We are not to disown our own issues or transfer them to others, but we are called to allow God to deal with our elements such as pride, superiority, and selfishness. Are these our thorns?

God's grace is sufficient. Receive it as the Great Potter and the Master Craftsman continue refining. Allow grace to hold you steady. Don't embrace a lifestyle of running, for you are destined to be a most magnificent masterpiece. God's ways are higher than ours.

*No fretting: God has **all the others** in His hands as well.*

They are receiving the graces;
they need to be with you while you are in process.

A Tee Shirt Message

*T*he Church has left the building. This pronouncement was seen adorned on the back of a tee shirt while in the marketplace. All people are walking billboards of one type or another. The Apostle Paul put it this way, *we are letters that are being written to be read.* Thus, the man who advertised so openly via his tee shirt about *being the church outside the building* had it distinctly right. His theology is a plumb line with Christ's, the Head of the Church.

Christianity 101: What and Where is the Church?

God settled the issue long ago, but people are slow at grasping and then retaining the truth over an extended period. The Old Testament records *The Ark*, a chest-like box, as literally or symbolically the place where *God's Holiness and Presence was to be* amidst His people. Where it went, God was. Next came *The Tent of Meeting.* It was a literal physical tent in which God met with His chosen. Finally, the magnificent temple constructed by Solomon and the lesser temples in grandeur were the next designated places for God's people to gather in and know His presence.

Moving forward into New Testament times, in which we live, and the unfolding of God's perfect ultimate plan, we understand God is now indwelling, tenting, abiding *in* His people by His Spirit. *Where the ark was, He was, and likewise now, where we are, He is.*

We must know that *we are* the temple of the Holy Spirit. *We are* ...

The buildings constructed of wood, tin, stone, mud, reeds, cement, or glass are not the holy places of reflection of God's glory. Once again, we are. Every day, everywhere we are, He is.

The church has left the building ... a long, long time ago. No building ever visited the hungry, clothed the naked, or prayed for the sick. If ever you begin to gaze upon a structure as the place of holiness and goodness, I trust you will remember the Tee Shirt message.

The Church Has Left the Building. It is simply echoing the Word of God that shouts ... you are and I am the Church, the temple in which God resides!

Go, be His hands of love and His voice of comfort to those He guides you to
... outside the building. You are the Church.
We are the Church who is being observed, and read, daily.
2 Corinthians

Yes, observed and read by others daily ... Most sobering.

Perceiving the Treasure

"*There was nothing attractive about him, nothing to cause us to take another look ... He embraced the company of the lowest ...*"

—Isaiah 53 (MSG)

This was written concerning Jesus. And now, for many around the world, it can also be said, *there is nothing about him or her, nothing to cause us to take another look.*

Ms. S, early forties and *never been kissed*, seemed just such a person. The sneers and jeers from the show's judges and audience alike were barely concealed as she stepped onto the stage. Her outward physical persona was one of a matronly looking woman, less than fashionably dressed, with a schoolgirlish voice when speaking, not fitting a woman her age. But then ... she opened her mouth, and an exquisite sound came forth in song, bringing all who were present to their feet in palpable amazement. The initial ridicule morphed swiftly into sounds and gestures of adoration. Doors of immense magnitude worldwide began rapidly opening to her, and eventually, her dream of singing before her Sovereign no doubt would become a reality.

Her story is yet to be fully known to the public at large, but what has already been gleaned is relevant to all times. We must let her story teach us and reach us deep within, for it is a story common to man.

There was nothing attractive about *Him*, nothing to cause us to take another look. Jesus was pelted, whipped, and mocked, made unrecognizable, disfigured in face. The sneers and jeers displayed by the Judges with Ms. S showcased the mindsets of many cultures. Like men of old, we demand that our kings, those we want to extol, follow, and adore, be of extreme magnificence and stand heads above others, like King Saul of biblical fame.

Ms. S's angelic voice did not just happen overnight. Since the age of twelve, she had been belting out love songs and church songs. Those who had known her in pubs and church alike saw and heard but did not perceive the magnitude of her gifting either. It almost, almost, happened again with thousands in attendance.

Yes, beauty is in the eyes of the beholder, and to some measure, talent is as subjective. We can simply say that we are products of our environs and let our base, mob-group mentalities take blame for our harsh and insensitive words and gesture manifestations *to other breathing, feeling, living human beings.* That is the way of the world, and we are certainly in the world. However, like one of Ms. S's three judges, I choose today to take full responsibility for my judgment by the outer cover that rears its ungodly, loathsome, lowly presence in my life on a more frequent basis than I would like to acknowledge. To gain a victory, I must shed the traits of judgment and face my biases in the light of day. Today is that day because Ms. S's story went live and, like an arrow, *pierced me in the process.*

I have judged and been judged in many spectrums. It is never right and is most often very painful.

This heroine-type had the graces and tenacity in life to endure. However, many others who have been jeered, sneered at, and bullied in some verbal or physical form have not. They wilted. They consigned themselves to be *less than* and, in a variety of ways, subsequently lost themselves. They self-aborted at times, with *our* known or unknown assistance.

Words and actions matter! Let us live this truth.

May my tears, and possibly yours as well, wash away the unacceptable judgments of today and years gone by. May the now-cleansed spaces within, by the power of God, be replaced with respect for all, regardless of preferences, statuses, or giftings.

As followers of Christ, we must respectfully say, *thank God for Jesus.* He took our penalties. As fellow travelers with those we have erroneously judged, we can confess, *"Forgive us, for we have not known what we have done."* And to our own inner core, we must have a dialogue and insist on change.

> *Someone's natural or spiritual life … may be in the balance.*
> *God, give us eyes and ears to perceive the treasure within.*

On the Judicial

It has been years, and I am still counting, since my dance commenced with the Judicial system that resulted from a work-related injury. The song is the same, but the movements to the dance have become more cumbersome and wearying, both in the natural and the spirit realm. However, my heart is now awakened.

One beautiful autumn day, I was off to work as usual. Hours later, a push, pop, and intense pain catapulted me into a dance with multiple strangers that had been assigned me. Being conscripted into this journey, I immediately was flung into a world of medical and legal wrangling that continues to astound. Many have gone this way before, as I had heard and read their stories, but there is nothing like walking through a fire to understand its components. I am now known as a number, a file number, and in the natural, there are faceless strangers who hold my care in their power.

My strength is not in the natural, for I am weakened. I stand weakened from physical pain and weakened from a position of unconscionable legal representation that allowed half-truths and innuendos to stand in a record without confrontation, stating in essence these things are small, thus inconsequential. I allowed my degreed counsel to take the lead in the dance, for, by schooling, he knew the legal symphony best. But he swiftly danced his way out when the realization became apparent that there would be no money settlement because I would not settle.

Instinctively, I knew my long-term medical needs, and the subsequent costs would trump any short-term monetary value they offered. In this, I did not bow or waver, although settling would have ended the wearying battle, at least momentarily.

My strength is to be in the spirit. But I had found myself weakened in the natural. Slowly, as the little foxes of innuendos got recorded in the legal system, so the little foxes of thought entered into my spirit man. Where is my God in this dance? Does He not know my tiredness? Does

He not care about truth reigning? Does He not care about my reputation with the faceless powers of a commission? Lord, You are known as the Advocate for the distressed, disenfranchised, and accused. They do not know me, and they do not know the whole truth. Yet, they continue to dance with the innuendos that they codified and lean on, making my truth of no value. God, my Omnipotent, Omniscient God, why does this dance continue? I am weak in spirit. My God, questions taunt me. They too are wearying.

And then, when the inner tears and rants ran dry from human exhaustion, a sudden word of knowledge is spoken from one of my treating physicians, "PK, don't let anyone intimidate you in this process," and at the sound, a ray of strength emerged from deep within. Someone knows. They believe the medical record of evidence holds truth that the judicial chooses to walk by due to the slothfulness of one of their own. Then in quietness, I dare to ask, *God, are you speaking?* The weariness is assuaged briefly as a note of rest in this musical score.

I end where I began. The dance continues. My weariness in both the natural and spirit ebb and flow as issues continue to gurgle up many years later, but I am stronger for having to endure this lengthy conscripted dance. The heat of the scorching fire is tangible, but as my head lifts without my effort, I cautiously open my eyes to see who is with me. Gazing through the smoke, I make out figures. Some are known, and others unknown. They are not high and lifted, wearing judicial robes, but they are seated on their knees making prayer intervention on my behalf. But then one appears quite different than all the others through the smoke. He is in white, and the aroma I catch is not of flesh being burned, but of life resurrected.

I give thanks, from the depths of my being, to the many individuals who, through prayer, were instruments of transformation in my fire. Renewal is coming ... for the dance that continues for all.

Prayer is Power.

Knock, Knock

*K*nock, knock. "Who's there?" I do not hear anything, so I ask again, "Who is knocking at my door?" I ask a little louder this time determined to hear who it is. But again, there is no response, nothing. Looking through my semi-covered window, I see no one. Yet, I know without a doubt that someone was knocking. I heard it distinctly. Nevertheless, I keep on keeping on with implementing my own ideas.

Tick-Tock goes the clock, and I find myself hours, days, and even years later, still wondering who is knocking at my door. The memories of the knocking do not fade, and the question continues to go unanswered as it happens again and again and again under different life circumstances. Then, at last, there is a dawning in my fog through a picture, a conversation, or a song … God. He is the One who has been knocking all along the way of my life. God.

Time

No more time to waste. The sounds sound more persistent and insistent than days gone by. The intervals seem shorter and more rhythmic. What is it, what is it God wants?

Frenzied, you run here, there, and everywhere asking what God could want, but to no avail. No one has the answer, or at least not your answer. *Tick-Tock* the clock of time continues. Panic wants to devour you, but you fight it off knowing it is not the answer. Then, one day, unexpectedly, fatigue arrives at the door of your thoughts uninvited, but you realize it just may bring the answer, not *be* the answer because you cannot run any longer, *you cannot run any longer!*

Then it is there, finally quieted and harnessed by lack of energy. The still small voice of God can finally be heard, dimly at first, as the remaining sounds of all the other voices fade away. At last, there is someone there, really there, accompanying the sound of the knocking. Weary, but no longer afraid, you invite Him in, and the conversation commences.

He begins with these words: *Come to Me all you who labor and are heavy-laden and overburdened, and I will cause you to rest {I will ease and relieve and refresh your souls} For my yoke is wholesome {useful, good-not harsh, hard, sharp, or pressing, but comfortable, gracious, and pleasant}, and My burden is light and easy to be borne.*

—Matthew 11:28, 30 (AMPC)

Indeed, in this hour, as we stand at the precipice of an unknown moment, with all its opportunities, possibilities, and potentialities, it is just the right time to yoke, or re-yoke, with the One who is and has and will be knocking.

Hear His voice and respond to the personal entreaty ...
Come walk with me, for I Am your way through and beyond.

All Time is Mine From The Womb to the Tomb through all of Eternity.
Come.

Facets of Love

*A*braham loved God enough that he was willing to sacrifice Isaac, his son, and literally placed him on an altar to slaughter him. **Genesis 12.**

God so loved the world that He gave His Son, Jesus, for the world, we are told. **John 3.**

Jonathon loved his friend David so much that he was willing to give him his rights to the throne. **1 Samuel 18.**

Naomi loved Ruth, and Ruth loved Naomi so much that they were bound to one another from hardship to hardship and nation to nation. *Ruth 1.*

Absalom loved power to such a degree that he tried to dethrone his father, King David. **2 Samuel 3.**

Jesus loved His mother, Mary, so much that, on the cross, He provided for her earthly care with John the beloved. **John 19.**

Paul so loved the gospel that chains and imprisonment were as nothing to him. **Acts 21-28.**

Esther's love for her people, the Jews, caused her to gamble on the graciousness of the king and enter his presence, without being sent for, knowing it could cost her life. **Esther 4.**

Esau's love of natural food caused him to casually forego his birthright, which was then bestowed upon Jacob because of it. **Genesis 25.**

Rachel was so loved by Isaac that when her father Laban fooled him on his wedding night by giving him Leah, Rachel's older sister, as his wife, he was willing to work for his father-in-law, yes, seven more years without pay to secure his real love, Rachel. **Genesis 29.**

King Herod Antipas loved Herodias, his brother's ex-wife, to the extent that he was willing to grant up to half his kingdom to her daughter who pleased him in dance. This love cost John the Baptist his head. **Matthew 14.**

The prophetess Anna loved God so much that she devoted her life to prayer. She could be found day and night in the temple. **Luke 2.**

Judas Iscariot, the betrayer, loved silver more than Jesus. **Luke 22.**

On and on, the Bible records or defines love for us in many facets. We experience human love as for family members, sexual love between man and woman, and love as found in special friendships and alliances. Love also is found in human appetites for food, drink, sleep, knowledge, wisdom, and a myriad of other objects. Money, power, and position are loved by many. We, as believers, are privileged to know a human love for God, which does not equal in any way His agape love, which is deep, constant, and never changing for His unworthy creation.

So love, whether defined as a strong, emotional attachment to a person or object, simple devotion, or the connotation of strength and steadfastness as in the Old Testament, is sometimes sentimentalized and very often overused in our day and age. We "love" everything! And it cheapens the true meaning of the word. We must still grapple with it.

What are you doing with love? How are you defining love? To whom or what are you showering your affections or devotions upon: Things, man, or perhaps even God?

It has been said, Love can be known from the action it prompts.

It needs to be asked: What actions are being prompted by your life?
Consider this statement. Consider your answer.

IX

TIMES OF CELEBRATION
AND SEASONS

IX

TIMES OF CELEBRATION
AND SEASONS

Holy Days. Holidays. Living Remembrances.

... Principles that transcend ...

On Hopefulness

*J*esus Christ is all about hope.

The blood and broken body are all about hope.

Today is all about hope, for His mercies are given new.

Why then are you not hopeful?

In the silence of this moment, tell Jesus why you are not hopeful.

And then listen as you gaze upon The Cross.

Releasing

With spring and new life in mind, I have had a great stirring to present a simple and practical word on which to meditate, and I have found it in the Book of Job. It is a principle in the Kingdom of God that dovetails beautifully with the Golden Rule. Living it will set in motion the hand of our God.

In the book of Job, we read, "And the Lord restored the fortunes of Job when he prayed for his friends ..." (See Job 42).

This is our nugget of wisdom: when we release prayers of good on the behalf of others, we release the goodness of our God toward ourselves as well.

It behooves us to note that these friends of Job had just completely and unabashedly assassinated his character. Nevertheless, God's principle and command was issued to Job to pray for them. *In his act of obedience, his life was transformed.* God is waiting for our prayers of goodness toward others, as he was Job's.

Today, if you hear the voice of the Lord in this, *be released in prayer* on behalf of others who have wounded you. It will rejuvenate and will set you on an expedition with the Lord that will unequivocally bring forth renewal.

He awaits your decision.

Loose Him. The dividends will be astounding.

Why Fear Death?

*P*roverbs 12 in The Book states: The path of the godly leads to life, so why fear death?

This is both a statement of truth and a question that each living person must come to terms with at some point in their lives.

As we approach the celebration of the birth of Jesus Christ it may do us well to contemplate the totality of his life circle that we may rejoice in a new fashion this Christmas season. To the children of Israel, and then to the church, the birth of Jesus was the beginning of God's path to life. Without His birth, there was no godly path. Without His physical death there was and is no hope for our eternal life. If we believe the Word of God and have received Jesus as the only way to meet with God the Father, why do multitudes of Christians fear death?

There is a disconnect in many that needs to be bridged and ministered to. Do we believe the Word of God? Do we really embrace and believe the tenets of our faith? If so, why fear?

The birth of Jesus was and is a time of rejoicing. The blood of Jesus is our covering, but the resurrection of our Lord is *our proof* that the path of the godly does lead to *life in the hereafter.*

If a loved one has died, causing a downcast spirit, re-read the Word of God and hear afresh what the angels proclaimed at Jesus' birth and at His tomb.

Fear Not ... for those who are in Christ Live On
(See John 11, John 14)

Live fully while on earth ... Fear Not!

The Holidays, A Word Fitly Spoken

"A word fitly spoken and in due season is like
apples of gold in settings of silver."
—Proverbs 25:11 (AMPC)

*H*oliday gatherings are traditional times to be with family and friends from far and near, whether in person or via telecommunications. Love and gaiety flow as freely as the Mississippi River. Yet, at times, tensions erupt because of the great diversity amongst peoples, often dampening a portion of the occasion. It only takes one lit ember to ignite a fire and only one voice singing loudly out of tune to spoil the song. Has it, ever, been you?

As a possible new tradition, ponder this: Conceivably, God wants you, yes you, to be the bearer of a word fitly spoken and in due season, a word that lifts, instructs, encourages, edifies, consoles, or even corrects. Although a spoken word is not wrapped and tied neatly with a bow in a conventional sense, this Proverb tells us that if it is fitly spoken, and in its due season, it will be like giving the gift of a golden apple in a silver setting.

Could there be anything more beautiful?

Be open to being God's bearer of a golden apple or two ...

in or out of the Holiday Season.

The Passion of Ms. B
The Grinch Cannot Touch Her Shoe Box

*H*er age is unimportant because it had nothing to do with the great light that penetrated through her perky brown eyes or the sing-song cadence of her voice as she emphatically and energetically promoted her passion to those about her without meaning to.

The conversation simply called it out of her. Ms. B began, "Do you know that this can be a year-long undertaking? It does not have to be done all at once, and it does not have to be done during the busy season. I watch for ads and go here and there looking for just the right things. The airlines, because of terror threats, have restricted the sending of some needed gifts like liquid soaps, and others do not like toy guns sent. Nevertheless, it can still be well done. Do you know, with an emphasis on *you*, that for twenty dollars, a child somewhere in the world who has nothing can be made to smile, at least for one day? Did you know that? Do you know you can send a picture or write a note, too? It does not take long. Can you just see the look of the little girl when she holds her first doll or the young boy who has a first ball to throw?" Without taking a breath or waiting for a reply, she states, "I can." Ms. B continues with her monologue, which takes her back many years to when she was a little girl. "Nothing for Christmas." *At least nothing child-like, was at the root of Ms. B's passion. No one will ever again have only an orange for Christmas if she can help it.*

Sitting near Ms. B was perhaps my most significant gift of all. I experienced a young girl who received little, but, because of it, she *determined to give much*. I sat beside *passion*. I *heard the thrill of passion. I smelled passion* and was enamored with the scent. *And now, I want to be passionate again.*

This is worthy of consideration. Has someone or some event entered your life slowly and insidiously, or abruptly and unexpectedly, and robbed you of a God-given passion? A thief comes to do just that. Jesus said,

"The thief comes to kill, steal, and destroy." He, she, they, or it simply come to seize what is yours.

Take Inventory

Is your love for God or others *dimming*? Has your zest for life left? Where have the times of dreaming gone? Are all the mountains too high to climb and the waters too vast to cross, even a mere pond? Is smiling a distant relative, or hope forever buried in the recesses of your being?

If so, hear the passion of Ms. B calling. Allow the past to catapult you forward and give you what has never been given to you, or has been stolen from you. Write the ending to your story in a new way. It is your story, after all. Do what is in your heart, and do it all year long. Believe you will be a blessing, just like Ms. B determined to be.

May the God of all creation permeate you
with His hope and power for your passions.

Dear Ms. B,

Although I did not capture your exact phraseology that evening at the church during the business meeting; I did capture your passion. You touched my life, and I thank God for it. Church business meetings are not my interest, but the one I attended with you was wonderfully profitable.

May Christmas and the New Year be days of wonderment for you, and may your personal shoe boxes (hearts desires) *ever be full* for the gifts of love you have so preciously passed on. The want of your little girl's heart has exponentially touched and filled so many others. May that knowledge warm you all year long. It will always warm me.

With warmth, PK

Silent Night, Holy Night

*D*o you see me? Lord, do you hear me crying? Do you not know that I am hungry, and I am thirsty, Father. Can't you see I need newness? I am looking tattered. The sheen and shine are gone. The soles of my shoes in the spirit have worn thin. My mind lacks peace and rest. I am dissatisfied; my whole being is demanding something new, something more. Hanging in and hanging on ... everything seems to be by a thread, Father. Are you there? Are you nearby?

Yes. It is as though I have finally slipped through the snare of the fowler to acknowledge I am in need. Too much time has passed since the internal quarreling began. My righteous torment has demanded a response. There is no longer any room nor time for further mental or spiritual gymnastics. One is or is not in need: Which is it? I have decided I am hungry, and I am thirsty. This is my truth. I am hungry for more of God and thirsty for more of Him. My spirit is crying, it is crying.

And, as though competing with my spirit's cry, are the racing thoughts of what is next, how will it turn out, what am I to do, where will it come from, is it over, should I hope, is there any hope?

Then I hear within me the words, *silent night, holy night,* as though in response to my inner cry and my mind's battle. The words *silent night, holy night* repeat again, deep within. They take my breath away in their still power. In rapid succession and for further fortification it seems, the words in *"quietness and trust"* come to mind from the book of Isaiah as well as *"He leads me beside quiet waters"* from the Shepherd's Psalm.

Truth is calling.
Will I respond to the remedy offered, the Word of God?

I say, "Yes, Lord. I say yes to your wooing and stirring of my spirit and soul once again, even as I look around to and fro for a physical sign you are here and have spoken. Alas, I experience no small voice in the whirlwind like Elijah, a burning bush like Moses, or a speaking ass as was under Balaam.

Yet, I hear myself say *yes*. In a smidgeon of time and wrapped in the mysteries of God, somehow a fresh deposit of resolve to hang in and hang on has presented itself. Cautiously, I acknowledge the trickling in of new hope, and as I do, the multitudes of fears that have been vying for my soul are slowly being quieted. Peace and good will touch me as I think all over again about the birds in the air, the grass and flowers of the field, and how much more adored and impeccably dressed I am and will be by my Father. Have I been promised fine linens now for my garments or is it righteousness, peace, and joy in the Holy One? My tears, too, I am reminded, even they are being kept in a bottle.

However, I am aware, that my great hunger and deep thirst persists. They are yet to be satisfied. But this too will serve God in this apparent season of aridness and famine. And I will continue to ask, seek, and knock. *He will* supply my strength. The one who is faithful and true will be faithful in His time and way. No longer will I find a surface rest, but I will find a *divine rest*.

It is a holy night ... for I
have been given fortitude in my evening.

"Silent night. Holy night. All is calm; all is bright. Sleep in heavenly peace." Sleep in heavenly peace repeats the song as though it is a command. Indeed, I will sleep well tonight. And you? It is for the asking.

Together, let us give thanks for Jesus Who is our hope and peace.

Mighty Counselor, Carole's Cast Stone

I have come that you may have life and with it my peace.
There now is no condemnation for those who are mine. —Romans 8

I ask, who will cast a stone? —John 8

*W*ho will cast a stone? A seasoned Christian with whom I have been closely acquainted and have admired for years shared a dream she had. In the first frame of the dream, she saw herself lying on the ground all alone. There was no one else present, and there were no sounds. She was simply lying there. As the image of her body lay still on the ground, she found herself rising, turning, and then looking back at herself on the ground, when she heard a gentle voice say, "Who will cast the first stone?" Immediately and systematically, *she then pummeled herself.* In agonizing rage and self-loathing, Carole's very own hands were the instruments used to hurl the stones. The dream ended abruptly.

The season of celebrating Christ's birth was upon us, and this dream is a poignant reminder as to the gifts that came to earth with Christ that clearly need to be unwrapped throughout our lives. Love, He Himself sent to us with the intent of reconciliation and instituted forgiveness as the tool through which we attain it. Once able to hurdle the great divide between man and God and man to man, we are left with perhaps the most difficult mission of all. The last mountain for many to climb is simply reconciling with oneself. For most, *self* is the cruelest, most unforgiving and relentless pursuer of one's dignity, with the outcome simply being condemnation. The voice of self-condemnation is a taskmaster no amount of love from others, nor even God, can overcome until one *willingly opens the door to hear* the still small voice say, "It is finished, it is finished, it is finished. The debt has been paid in full. You are free. All is forgiven. Come now and drink deeply from the well of salvation." —Isaiah 12

Accept the gift, open the gift, and receive the gift of forgiveness for yourself offered by Christ. Allow the same mercy you extend to others, be yours. Let today be the day you earnestly begin to forgive yourself for every wrong choice and decision you believe you have made in life.

Dare to open the most marvelous gift
that stands at the door of your heart ...

Forgiveness

The Queen, A King, Young Mary, and A Child King

Act 1 - The Queen

*M*any years ago, a woman pushed to the brink did a daring thing. She entered the court of her King Xerxes without first being invited in. This action should have cost her life, but it did not. Instead, the following happened. The king was on his throne facing the entrance when he noticed Queen Esther standing in the court, and he was pleased to see her. Following established protocol, the king extended the gold scepter in his hand, which was the royal invitation to legally approach him. In response, Esther walked forward and touched the tip of the scepter, also following protocol. The king asked, "And what is your desire, Queen Esther? What do you want? Ask and it is yours, even if it is half my kingdom!"

—Esther 5 (MSG)

This king of so many years ago met the queen in her audacious dare. In lieu of public ridicule, rebuke, and banishment from his kingdom at the least, and more probable the death penalty, an unthinkable invitation of extraordinary proportion was extended to this woman named Esther. Graciousness beyond understanding was granted as one half of this earthly king's vast empire was offered to her. Imagine the power. Consider the opulence. This, however, was not why she presented herself before the king. It was not in self-interest but for freedom, liberty, and *literal life for a people group condemned to extermination* by this very monarch due to another's deception. The risk was taken for the queen's own people., the Jews. They could live only by the proclamation of the king. It was granted.

A king humbled himself for a woman, and that same woman saved a nation because of "her King."

Time rolls on. Fast forward many, many more years.

Act 2 - Young Mary and A Child King

A monumental earth- and life-changing event that had been foretold but often disbelieved, mocked, and scorned is now unfolding before multiple people groups. The time had come for the King of all kings and Lord of all lords to make His debut. As prophesied, He arrived lowly in a stable. With word of the impending birth, the ruling king, Herod, was so angry and jealous he ordered this baby to be found under false pretenses so that he could have him exterminated. However, this did not happen according to this human king's timetable, for one greater and grander had another plan. This was and is an unearthly, other-worldly plan that confounds multitudes to this day.

"The Word became flesh and blood and moved into the neighborhood. We saw the glory with our own eyes, the one-of- a-kind glory, like Father, like Son, generous inside and out, true from start to finish." (John 1:15 MSG)

This King of the Jews, this Jesus, was born to a young woman named Mary who gave herself freely and selflessly to her God, bringing shame upon herself, though she did nothing personally wrong. She simply trusted. *Unmarried, young Mary should have quietly been put away as a solution to the pregnancy,* her young fiancé thought. Yet, neither did this happen. This God, who acquiesced to be born of flesh, humbled Himself to become a man to identify fully with His people. The King of all kings emptied Himself of all power and entrusted Himself to a young woman. Unthinkable. He exchanged a Glory beyond human comprehension for a season to be the Living Scepter who offers an eternal graciousness to His people. The battle still rages surrounding His Lordship-Kingship. A young woman surrendered herself to bring forth a Child King. It was daring. She is now called Blessed. A jealous King Herod attempted to annihilate the Child King Jesus. He showed no mercy nor grace, as Herod was all about self-kingdom and glory. He did not ultimately succeed.

In summation, Esther who in time became a queen *prevailed* in Act 1. *She dared* to throw herself on the mercy of her king, and life was granted for the multitudes. Similarly, years later, a young Mary's *trusting yes,* Act 2, brought forth the plan of salvation who is Jesus *and through Him the restoration of God and His people.*

Time continues to roll on. Fast forward many, many more years. It is now today.

Act 3 - You, I, and An Eternal Signature

As the year draws to a finale, and Christians around the world celebrate God's graciousness toward them, they, in turn, all of His people, need to have the courage to be selfless, like Esther and Mary. Let us go tell this story of yesterday, today, and forever.

Come lowly all … the Gift of Love awaits.
And know that when the Prince of Peace moves into your neighborhood
and is given dominion, the landscape of your life is forever changed.
It is God's Signature.

In Remembrance of The Apple

*I*t was a gift, this red apple, not for decoration or show, but for consumption was the apple given. For days I walked around it, pondered it, and looked at it. I held it and even twirled it by the short grayish stem as I continued believing it was not the real thing. Then the time to go back over the mountain again came, and with the apple beside me for a hundred miles, with a peek here and there, I still could not get myself to accept as true that it was the red delicious variety my friend of years stated it was. Absent was the deep coloring, slim shape, height as well as weight that I came to believe was the trademark of a genuine Red Delicious apple. Days later, around the eleventh hour, a desire for something sweet overcame me. Rooting around to satisfy it, I found little to choose from. It was only then that I begrudgingly tasted the gift that was given many days before.

And this, too, was a gift but of a different type. In a garden thousands of years ago, God made a tree that would produce fruit. This fruit was such that it beckoned mankind. The attractiveness exceeded righteousness. What was forbidden was chosen. The fascination with the fruit overcame a specific God direction, "Do not eat of. …" But then the allure …

Now the serpent was more crafty than any beast of the field which the Lord God had made. And he said to the woman, "Indeed, has God said, 'You shall not eat from any tree of the garden?" The woman said to the serpent, "From the fruit of the trees of the garden we may eat; but from the fruit of the tree, which is in the middle of the garden, God has said, 'You shall not eat from it or touch it, or you will die." The serpent said to the woman, "You surely will not die! For God knows that in the day you eat from it your eyes will be opened, and you will be like God, knowing good and evil." When the woman saw that the tree was good for food, and that it was a delight to the eyes, and that the tree was desirable to make one wise, she took from its fruit and ate; and she gave also to her husband with her, and he ate. Then the eyes of both of them were opened, and they knew that they were naked; and they sewed fig leaves together and made themselves loin coverings. They heard the sound of the Lord God walking in the garden in the cool of the day, and the man and his wife hid themselves from the presence of the Lord God among the trees of the garden. Then the Lord God called to the man, and said to him, "Where are you?" He said, "I heard the sound of You in the garden, and I was afraid because I was naked; so I hid myself". And He said, "Who told you that you were naked? Have you eaten from the tree of which I commanded you not to eat?"

—Genesis 3 NASB

These two pieces of fruit, both given as gifts thousands of years apart, teach a similar story: A story of deception. Relying on natural sight and personal experience alone, without believing a trusted friend's voice of knowledge, caused a genuine piece of fruit to be branded as an imposter and the giver of the gift in tandem to be identified as uninformed. In the Garden, the gift of communion with God was distorted, disrupted, and diminished, and broken by the seduction of physical beauty and loveliness. The submission to, or guidance from, an imposter's voice was willingly embraced to partake of the desire of the natural eye.

Perhaps the next time you vacillate between choices, you will come into remembrance of The Apple. It may make the difference between life and life more abundantly. All that glitters, sparkles, and displays as authentic is not always authentic. On the other hand, the unimpressive, indecorously-packaged may merely be the covering for the unimaginably beautiful.

Think the Cross. Think the Apples. Consider them.

Pick Up Your Cross

*T*he cold and overcast skies of winter are slowly fading and giving way to clearer skies, budding nature, and warmer breezes. Spring signals new life. Hope is in the air.

At around the same time, Christians of every tribe and tongue flock to their places of worship to commemorate the Cross of Christ. The tensions of solemnity and triumph are palpable as dance, song, and liturgy are interwoven according to each gathering's tradition.

Man-God Jesus rode lowly on a donkey toward His life's ultimate purpose, The Cross. This would be the means of the shedding of His blood over all of humanity for life eternal, regardless of how many ultimately accept His act of love. In His final moments on earth as Man-God, eternity records these three words: *"It is finished,"* followed by burial and then resurrection. No one perceived as a "God," or self-crowned as a "God" before, since, or to the present day has ever been able to accomplish what Jesus did, and that is His return from the dead and ascension to His place of origin.

The Misconception of Exemption

The cross ... "Pick up your cross and come follow me" is a foundational, yet little embraced, truism of the Christian faith for many. It is glossed over for the more palatable parts of the faith, such as healing, health, vigor, and wealth. The prevailing attitude is to have no difficulties in any realm: Where trial and tribulations exist in the form of abject poverty or severe illness, to name a few, they are considered for those less mature, less dynamic, less knowing concerning their *rights in the faith.* Often, to serve God is to assume exemption from the hardships of life. Yet, this is untruth. The call found in scripture to *pick up one's cross* is all inclusive. There are no noted, defined people exemptions. The Word of God reports trials of kings and governors, children, widows, priests, the poor, and *People of the Way*. It is all inclusive. Therefore, the misconception or mistaken belief of exemption from the human conditions and experiences on earth is patently false, whether unintentional or a deliberate embrace of false teaching.

The Easter narrative is to bring to the fore again the impartiality and lack of prejudice the Man-God Jesus personifies. It continues to be the greatest story ever told. If, in this springtime, you or a loved one are in a season of suffering and adversity, look toward the Cross and perceive truth. See hope. Know you are not and will not be forsaken. Let no voice, yours or any others, define you as a failure. Was Christ on His Cross?

*Can we hear the living God say **pick up your cross and come follow me?***
*Can we hear Him say **no disciple is above his teacher***
nor a slave above his master?
(Matthew 10, John 15)

An Easter Thought,
The Worth of Blood

Whatever is True
Whatever is Noble
Whatever is Right
Whatever is Pure
Whatever is Lovely
Whatever is Admirable
If anything is Excellent or Praiseworthy

Think about such things.

—Philippians 4:8 (NIV)

*F*or this exercise of thought is under our control and, if practiced as a discipline, will take us from darkness into light.

Remembering Always: It took The Cross to Dispel Darkness, Forever.

May Jesus receive back To Himself , from our lived lives, every drop of His blood's worth.

Yes, Every Drop of His Blood's Worth ... From Me, From You.

Easter: A time to remember.
Every day: A moment in time to respond to His sacrifice.

"If anything is excellent or praiseworthy, think about such things."

X

CHAPLAINCY
A Clinical Pastoral Residency

X

CHAPLAINCY
A Clinical Pastoral Residency

Hospital Settings: Life and Death,
A World of Its Own

Called to mature and stand where I never envisioned: Chaplain Residency, life amid Trauma.

Chaplaincy in a clinical setting is a world of its own. Steeped in trauma and called to walk with those often in the depths of tragedy, it held an awakening for me personally to the graces given to those who choose and are gifted to meet the needs of the cries of the human body and the subsequent ramifications. Hospitals are places where hope ebbs and flows with life given and life taken with a rapidity that transcends human capacity at times. To all those who have dedicated themselves to the human condition within the walls of a clinical setting … truly you heard a divine calling.

It was a humbling within and without.

The following *Mini's* are personal excerpts of a few encounters that touched me deeply along the way in my residency. They represent a small cross sampling of encounters that, in the role of a hospital chaplain, are not unusual, day in and day out. In no manner are they complete.

Due to HIPPA regulations, I share these reflections based on real people with real circumstances without divulging identifiable personal information.

The Harp, a Prophetic Voice

*Music Therapy is a tool used often in Chaplaincy settings.
The Harp was written out of my heart response to an encounter
with a Harpist during residency.*

I could not see the face, but the fingers stroked, plucked, and glided ever so gracefully creating melodious, harmonious ethereal sounds. They took me away, singularly transported conscious me into a day gone by, two, even three … time was enveloped, time simply evaporated, or was it I?

Yes, I was involuntarily, unexpectedly taken by notes, not words, spoken ever so gently by a chief counselor's voice.

What was removed? Moreover, what was replaced, perhaps even from my face?

I still do not know what was banished, conceivably added to, in my very human file space.

No, I cannot quite say. It is yet to be revealed.

Yet to be revealed, but I know, yes, I know, it will not forever be concealed.

Timing in life; timing in music … much counting to do.

Harpist play on, you know not what you do.

Harpist play on, as healer, deliverer, and peace maker more.

Harpists play on … your strokes reach deep into various facets of one's core.

Please harpist … play on.

For your voice is prophetic, and it is not by your choice.

Harpist play on for many a score …

The Voice of Three,
Women in Differing Circumstances

Patients: Cancer, Multiple Sclerosis, Son Attempted Suicide

Mom with Cancer

"*C*haplain, my body is weakening from cancer. It is. I do not want to die yet." I listened, listened, listened intently. Few words from me: Less was better today. She needed an ear, and it was not for trivial matters or for self-aggrandizement, or for sport. She was in a deep place with self and God. I am thankful it was my ear. I had the opportunity to experience power in presence.

She shared a heavenly encounter that occurred in childbirth years before, stating it was a beautiful and most peaceful place. She had desired to stay there but was not allowed. Even though she was in the process of birthing a long-desired child, heaven outshone bringing forth new life on earth. Years later, and now in financial poverty and experiencing physical and emotional hardships of great magnitudes, she stated she wanted to stay on earth and live more years. Further detail was left unspoken that day for she abruptly fell asleep, most likely from the high-powered medicines being dripped into her veins.

It seemed so incongruent with her earlier life's desire. She experienced what many dream of, seeing heaven while on earth, and now wanted no part of it. What was it about impending death, that seemingly obliterated what she painstakingly spent much of her time talking with me about concerning her heavenly visitation? I was left to hold the conundrum…

So Aware and Multiple Sclerosis

"Multiple Sclerosis is taking my life. It is taking my life and taking my mind." Having many previous conversations, I had not heard this kind of talk before from *So Aware*. I can only listen now, heavy of spirit, as she has captured my heart personally. She was vibrant of spirit in our first encounters, ready to hurdle any bar as in times past as an athlete.

And then a short period of time elapsed until we met again. This time, her lamp was dimmed, her speech was almost unintelligible, she could not stand nor hold her head up.

I wrestled with what would be ministerial. What? I concluded with presence. Most sacred presence be fitting. Sacred relationship that we built, hold: Am I rightly equipped for this turn in stage, I wondered. No play by play to go by. I wanted to get it right for my sister. She felt like a sister. She felt like sister. Was I good enough to be called sister. It was a later, lonely contemplation.

Mother, Dark Eyes, and Six Words, Son Attempted Suicide

"Pray God … Pray God my son." Looking down at this diminutive woman and directly into her pleading dark eyes, touching her arm gently after hesitating, wondering if it would be acceptable to do so, and at the same time, reiterating, reinforcing her request was done. Yes. Yes, I have, and I will. This, too, seems enough for chaplain words. No more needed today. They would presumably get in the way. Prayer is what *mom* wanted. Prayer is what she received. Personally, I received something else. I went somewhere different today. I went into the depths of another's despair. I heard it. I felt it in only six words. Forget why the prayer was needed. Forget this is her second time walking with a son who viciously violated himself, violated family. The family dynamics, the systems pale today. Forget it … do not probe it … no need to understand any more. His mother was what mattered. She was the patient. And with my yes on prayer, I saw a flicker of relief in her face, and her body seemed to relax. Time was calling. I left *Pray God* standing outside her son's room gazing in, which was just as I found her shortly before, *but perhaps not so alone.*

Reflection on The Voices of Three Women

The voices of these women continue on in me. Life continues. Many others have come and gone, yet these encounters echo within as though I am encased in glass. Each person and family are facing earthquake-size trials. Today, I do not want to identify them as losses; it seems so final in some way, and this chaplain needs to believe for more for them and for me. Together now, in unison, it is no longer a trio of voices, but add mine as fourth. God, where are You? Will You send a miracle, sustain life, and keep on earth?

Help us … These cries are deep, and they are not to man. Man is simply the touchable, knowing the answers needed lie beyond human capabilities and capacities.

I muse, in all our wisdom, we dance as on a pinhead, with our knowledge, and there is no overflowing. There are no crowded conditions there. How we deceive ourselves, and every now and then, our educated ways come back in waves of stench saying, "No, what you do know is simply infinitesimal." There are universes more, and our knees bow again.

Where are the philosophers and the sages of our times? They are in the end as mystified. Where are the chaplains that can answer *their God cries*? Consider Job's friends who cruelly pelted him with accusatory language, stating he was in the circumstances of unimaginable loss due to his own sin. *God help us all, should we be found serving up, no matter how seemingly efficient and gracious, even science-based thrice double-blinded studies, our beliefs, and thoughts upon anyone in the depth of their despair.*

God please … let this truth be my daily bread. And, sisters, please forgive me if I have not been enough as chaplain on your behalf. In process, in process.

Alone But With Faithful Friends

First Day-First Assignment
Adult Intensive Care

*T*he Hospitalist Doctor was waiting for my arrival. He proceeded to share the circumstances unfolding in Room 12. It was determined that John Doe was in the end stages of life; his body was shutting down from a life of alcoholism. Palliative care was ordered. No other life-sustaining measures would be utilized. The Doctor estimated he had perhaps a few hours to live.

Standing outside the door and gazing in, the room looked bright and airy, defying the somberness of the occasion presented. John Doe was covered with a sheet-blanket, with a simple blue oxygen mask over his mouth and nose. Moving closer to his bed allowed me to glimpse the largest set of blue eyes I have ever seen. They were wide open, with a glaze cast over them staring straight ahead. There were no noticeable body movements other than the rhythmic breathing with his chest rising and falling as he inhaled and exhaled. It was both haunting and peaceable.

In hushed tones and away from the bed, a husband and wife, who were John's friends, began sharing his story: "We tried calling him for a few days, but when he didn't answer, we finally went to his rented room. We found him on the floor, unconscious. John is not going to make it. He has had a hard life. No friends but us that we know of. No family that we know of. He lived a life of social isolation and did not easily engage with people, but rather talked about his *primary relationships being with nature and, in particular, his love for the ocean.* John was nice but angry. He never really said why. He lived in very run-down conditions, and often we gave him food and drove him to clothing closets when clothes or shoes were needed. *He was our friend, and he was good to us, too.*" The mutuality of relationship seemed particularly important for this couple to share with me. They *were not simply Good Samaritans, but they had relationship that mattered to them. John was not less than but fully equal to …*

They then asked me, with tears running down their cheeks if I would pray. They were Christians and worshipped within the Baptist tradition. Neither knew if John had accepted Jesus as his Savior, and this was their present pain.

As requested, we gathered around his bed. I held hands with both John and his friends. Inwardly. I quieted and yet simultaneously wondered how to be a bridge of life in this *trio's hour of need.* Yes, trio. The prayer: "God, thank you that John was found by his loving friends. Thank you for John's friendship toward them. We thank you for the ocean and breezes that John delighted in and took comfort from and which we believe you created. Together now, we are asking for your mercies and asking that John could again experience the sand between his toes and the ocean breezes on his cheeks. We entrust him to your mercy, your care. We thank you that you have known and understood everything about John's life, knowing exactly why he traveled the paths he did.

John, now may you know without question God's purpose, presence, and peace. It's just the two of you. Respond to His call. Father, we commit him into your love, and in Jesus' name, we pray."

John's breathing seemed to quiet down after this simple but heartfelt prayer. Within ten minutes, not hours, John breathed his last, but not alone, with husband-and-wife friends by his side.

Psalm 139
I formed you in your mother's womb ...
I knew every day of your life before there was one ...

The Rev. and The Need to Confide

*T*he bespectacled, Rev. was stretched out on his bed seemingly not in great distress at the time I met him. I knocked on a partially open door, introducing myself as the chaplain on duty for the day in the Emergency Department and stating your nurse thought you may want a visit. "Yes, yes, please, come on in."

He was quite pale and appeared somewhat thin in his face but not fragile in appearance. He had an inviting southern tone, and he was sharp of mind. The Rev. watched closely as I came toward his bed and then warmly extended his hand to me.

After a brief greeting, he began to fill me in with generalities about his life as a minister, husband, and father. The deeper issue of his heart was then addressed. The Rev. stated, "I have not really talked about it with anyone." The man was overcome with welling emotion. His chest rising as if to keep the uncontainable contained. His body tightened. His eyes were moist, and his lips quivered.

"It is hard. You just do not share something like this with everybody, but I want to talk about a son." He continued rapidly, "My son likes men and has for many years. He lives with one presently." The Rev. continued sharing his heartache, and I simply listened. "He would not tell his mother he was gay. He wanted me to do it. It took me years. How was I going to do that? I could not get the words out. I could not hurt my wife. I loved her, and she was so gentle. I did not have the heart to tell her. Eventually, I tried to address the subject with my wife, but it was as though she knew what I needed to say. She would not go there with me. She did not want to know." Finally, the Rev. cried, and cried some more very softly.

Reflection

I was in the presence of a God-fearing, loving, elderly man who was not able as yet to bridge with a prodigal son, nor a son with his father, because of the tensions within both of them due to choices concerning lifestyles. Homosexuality and the church are one of the great issues of our times. Regardless of anyone's personal philosophy, the intensity of feelings on each side of the aisle is deep and wide.

I chose not to assign blame, guilt, or judgment to either party for continuing the separation and can only believe the son is as wounded emotionally as his father. Additionally, the Rev. shared that his son is carrying the torment of HIV in his body and soul.

In ending, I asked if he would like me to pray, which was answered in the affirmative. I had no unction to pray for the Rev.'s presenting physical issues, nor the son's. The only prayer within me was for reconciliation. I prayed with a heavy heart over the pain of their separation. Yet, at the same time, I had great confidence in God's ability to soften and draw together this father and son.

The depth of despair and brokenness on multiple layers in this Elder's story pierced me.

At the end of our time together, I was affirmed as "his minister," with the additional comment I needed to remember, "Ministers need ministering to."

He also gave me a word that he believed was from God and his number if I ever wanted to be in touch. I took the number knowing I would not. Our time was complete, and I was becoming more comfortable with this knowledge ever so slowly. **Time complete.**

Always lessons to be learned and compassion to be worked in.
Reconciliation is attainable. Reconciliation heals the broken hearted.

Do you need to be reconciled with someone? Consider the query.

Wife Invisible, The Pain of Her Lover Husband

A Med-Surge Unit, Private Waiting Room

*I*t was a Friday morning after a night on call, and I was just getting ready to tackle some notes acknowledging several families' deaths when I received a page to go see a family who had themselves just experienced a death. After initial and numerous introductions, I found myself on my knees in front of the patriarch of the family and husband of the deceased. The reason became clear in time.

Reflection

The facial muscles on his thin but strong frame were visibly taut as he began to share what it had been like for twenty-plus years of their married lives. His wife had been vivacious, gregarious, and had many friends until having a stroke. Lover-Husband painstakingly related how lifetime friends, after a few post stroke visits, abruptly stopped visiting. When shopping or dining out in their small community, no one ever stopped to talk with them, or even look their way, as they once did. "It was like she was invisible; she wasn't there; she just didn't exist. I could not stand it for her. Other than family, no one took the time to talk with her. She was not dumb. She just had a hard time getting her words out."

He was just talking, not looking for any answers or feedback. It was as though a dam had been released. "I haven't talked this much to anyone."

The stories flowed in and out and all about on multiple family topics revolving around his wife and the rather large family clan, including his wife's beloved dog who had stayed faithfully by her side until its recent death. One more loss, I thought, in the pool of so many others. As the conversation was about to conclude, the family patriarch shared one last appalling event concerning a visit they had from a local minister soon after his wife's stroke. "He sat in my home and told me if I didn't join his large church, I was going to hell."

"I had had enough. Enough! I know God didn't leave us, but people did."

Our time together was now coming to an end after a few hours. The son walked with me to the door and said in a quiet voice as I was leaving, "This was amazing. My dad has not allowed anyone to pray or talk about God with him since Mom's stroke. When I saw you get down on your knees in front of my dad, I could not believe it. He just opened up. I have never seen him do that before. Thank you so much." He gave me a last hug. "My life has been changed today." And so had mine. I would never be the same, whether in ministry or human service positions.

It was humbling that Lover-Husband, after many years of chosen non-contact with any minister, allowed this chaplain in for prayer and conversation. I was righteously angered for the treatment that he and his Invisible Wife endured at the hands of friends and strangers alike after her stroke. I was equally angry at a man, let alone a pastor, who had the audacity to suggest a person come to his church or go to hell. I was relieved and believed with the grieving Lover-Husband that his wife was now at peace and whole. I was moved by the son who had confided he lost but re-found his "heart" professional moorings because of the love shown to his mother by staff in the last days of her life. He was determined to be again the man of heart and compassion he once was.

I continue to be intrigued by the instincts and unconditional devotion of animals toward their human families. Truly, they too are ministers to the lonely and disenfranchised.

Lastly, I celebrate the role of Pastoral Care. This family's story underscored the call, the need, and the benefit of a holistic approach within the walls of a clinical setting.

Medicine alone could not touch this family's fundamental needs in their grieving process. It took diversity in team.

The heartache, sadness, and pain resulting in such palpable isolation inflicted because of people's uncomfortableness with disabilities needs to cease. I was pricked to my core, saddened, and ashamed for anyone I had walked by because of my own lack of knowledge and my own discomforts. I was both honored and corrected that day in another's time of deep sorrow.

It reminded me again that teachability and usability go hand in hand. May we embrace correction when it is due. It is becoming in the sight of God.

At Their Own Hands

One Female, One Male

$\mathcal{Q}$ was called to the Emergency Department to be present for the arrival of two unrelated families, with similar circumstances, who did not yet know their loved ones had died. One at her own hand, one at his own hand. The reflection is an interweaving of both.

Reflection on Suicide, At Their Own Hands, Two on The Same Day

Whose perspective counts on the day an individual decides to end life not only for themselves as they have known it, but for all those who are intimately and even loosely intertwined? Whose perspective counts today? An ashen-faced elderly father whose wife had died recently. The sobbing sibling who pounded her fists on a chaplain's back while being held? Or the concerned supervisors who went to check on an absentee employee and found a very bloody body? What about the vomiting wife, staring blankly like a deer frozen by the glare of headlights, talking about being showered with gifts and a love kiss prior to hearing the fatal shot? Perhaps the son who met his father's fatal violence with a fist through a wall creating a trickling of blood and damage that would never equal the finality of a bullet. Or the solemnity of a daughter who was robotically all about the family business of public relations as her boyfriend's body trembled at the news? Perhaps he was reacting for both. The brother, as well, did not shed a tear, but his girlfriend may have cried for both.

The hospital needed a signature in exchange for a few personal belongings. That is all she had on arrival. *"The bracelet should go to her daughter." "Would you like his boots? They are quite bloody. I will need you to sign for them."* I understood the need for accountability, but what a seemingly frigid system. A life is gone, a signature is required. The exchange seems absurdly untimely. Business in the immediate midst of death. Whose perspective counts?

Suicide is the final, the ultimate great escape for one and the beginning of a new journey that will not be forged easily by most of the victims, family, and friends. *The why of "At Their Own Hands" actions, will be delegated to the maybe this or maybe that, or the if only pile of human waste files that are found in all.* On the other hand, the police, medical, and coroners' reports will be succinct. Died of self-inflicted wounds in particular places of their bodies, with specific implementations. "No dad, her boyfriend wasn't involved. A note was found." Cases closed.

The survivors will replay repeatedly the phrases *maybe, if only, we would have, or should have.* The record began immediately from spouses, parents, children, siblings, and friends as though they were all reading from the same book of guilt lines, especially for such occasions. The similar refrains were haunting, and if embraced too tightly, it would lead to their own emotional deaths in part. They must hear, hear, and hear it was not their fault, not their fault!

This is a legacy no one deserves.

How we walk with those who survive the carnage of another's ultimate choice is holy ground.

As I was preparing to leave the Emergency Department, a male nurse asked from a spiritual perspective, "Chaplain, what do you think happens when a person commits suicide? Some people believe they are going to hell." Yes, I am aware of this thought process, but I believe we must always entrust these circumstances to the mercies and omniscience of God. He alone knows the capacities of each of us, in all circumstances and seasons of our lives. Ultimately, and only God knows who is truly His, I rest in these truths. Perhaps you will as well.

Immediately following, the Junior Nurse asked, "How did I do? Did I do a good job? I'm not used to this." She had just shared with me a few days prior that she was in training for the trauma rooms and was not sure how she would do. It was a good ending, after a trying time we shared together, to be able to say, "You could not have been more professional, respectful, kinder with the families. You will be exceptionally good." She had an abundance of up-to-date medical knowledge, which was woven into a young servant's heart. She was beautiful to observe that day, as a budding young medical provider amid others' deep darkness. In fact, she was more than good; she was stellar. Her light in the hands of God will become ever brighter.

The family pastor walked with me into the hallway after I spoke with the staff. He interjected, as though he was aware of the battle within me: "Thank you for your service to God's people here. Thank you. Tell others you work with, thank you. This is important work."

I knew this was genuine, yet, could I receive it? Life and death, stillness, and life: I am trying to figure out life and death during this moment of time, recalling the words the seasoned nurse said to me while preparing the deceased to be viewed by their respective families. "Breasts, face, and eyelids lifted. Diamonds gifted. Does not satisfy, does it?"

*Human pain. Human suffering. God, you promised, one day, there will be no more tears, no more sorrow. Today just was not that day. Gift us with the **want to**, to live ... when ours has taken flight.*

Decidedly, chaplaincy is a most valuable ministry,
but, the question remained, was it for me?

Reflection On Baby Z

A Maternity Birthplace

*A*gain, I know, more equates to less in words, and presence rules the day. Quietly being with sadness and sorrow, the depth I know not of, seemed so sufficient and so insufficient. Watching a mother who knew life in her first-born child, now holding stillness in a newborn. I could not find feeling within. Looking at this miniature, created being wrapped and dwarfed in pink, and blue, and white in his mother's arms, being caressed, kissed, and studied, and then handed into my arms to be handed into the nurse's arms who would then hand him off again, in the natural, to a funeral home.

I was ever grateful for believing in a living. loving, omniscient God, as did Baby Z's parents.

Mom and I met in conversation wherever she wanted to go, explain, or explore that day. We went to her home, into the family dynamics, hopes, and dreams for a daughter to have a little brother, to social work co-workers and the seeming injustice of her loss versus the giveaway mentality of so many other mothers, clients she worked with.

I was anxious for this mom. She wanted no reminders. She wanted the scene of her home to be cleansed by the baby's father, before she arrived. No crib. No gifts. No sad family members or friends present. She had *no life* to take home that day *nor enough life within* her to converse.

She talked, I listened. She cried, I held her, knowing no matter how many items were physically removed from her home, her journey had no one-day make over. That was for Hollywood. Her scar and pain from the cesarian section had already told her what the mind could not yet take in.

I was privileged to pray, to dedicate, to entrust their little one to their God and my God.

I was so grateful my theology had no woulds and shoulds concerning babies that some other chaplains were bound by. This was the ultimate gift for a mother that a chaplain on duty could give, despite some denominations' tenets on innocent babies that I did not embrace. This was *the beginning of letting go, and not just to nothingness but to their God.* Dedicating Baby Z met the desire of broken human hearts, and my name was joined on a certificate with baby, mom, dad, and of course, the institution. That day was noted, in eternity, wasn't it? God's Word says so. Nothing transpires on earth that He does not see or know.

Finally, some emotion. Delayed, but now present. I was alive, evidenced by my own quiet tears as I collected myself in the privacy of the pastoral care office. As I looked to my left, I saw the Children of The World mobile twirl as though more than just me and the Blues playing on the radio were present. It was only three o'clock in the afternoon. I already had two deaths in conjunction with multiple family, friends, and staff to minister to. It was just the beginning of a long twenty-four hours in the hospital that day ...

A baby's death leaves a valley full of questions in its wake.
It remains mystery.

Father, give us Your comfort, Your strength.
We are never enough in and of ourselves ...

Dealing With No

*M*r. No was on a stretcher, parked in the emergency department corridor, dressed in typical street clothing, which consisted of jeans, a plaid shirt, and casual shoes when I encountered him. No one was with him. Routinely, I acknowledged anyone in the hospital corridor, and today would be no different. The response however would be.

Trying to make light of the surroundings, I introduced myself as the chaplain and continued with a lighthearted comment for the privacy the hospital afforded him, and that elicited a smile. "What brings you here today? Heart?" "I have been having chest pains and wondering if I had a heart attack." He said it rather nonchalantly, and I wondered if I would be that collected in his position, or was it bravado on his part? "Waiting to have some tests and for my wife to arrive." Is there anything I can assist you with? Are you a person of faith? Perhaps say a prayer? "No, I don't have any beliefs like that. No." And with that single emphatic, but polite, perhaps slightly clipped response, I knew our brief encounter was complete, and I responded with the absolute best to you.

Reflection

This "no" response had not often happened to me during chaplaincy, but I can vividly recall the first time and the absolute blindsided, disconcerting, emotional effect it had on me, although I had been a minister for years. A standard component of Clinical Pastoral Education is the individual case discussions each resident presents to the entire group for critique. After sharing my brief Mr. No encounter, immediately a reproving declaration by a fellow resident followed, "PK, when you enter into a room, you should be ready for anything." He was absolutely correct, notwithstanding this wisdom came from the youngest and least ministerially-seasoned person in the room.

This day, however, the resounding "No" did not penetrate me to the core as the first. Did I anticipate it? I absolutely did not! *What then made the difference*, I wondered. Perhaps just one word, just as powerful as No, met me: Experience. Coupled with experience is the deeper embrace of not owning another's decision, realizing the no is targeted at a much larger frame than my own, birthed out of a differently based philosophy.

Would I have liked a different relational meeting with this patient? Yes. But the door was closed, even in a hallway. Did I meet the patient's need? Yes, by cordially parting and accepting his voice as valid. Has God met my need through this encounter? Yes, through the mystery of being changed.

With this truth, I moved on to the next patient, and the next, aware that at any time, I may well hear no again. And I tell you today, I may or may not react the same. Nevertheless, I have been expanded.

The path of growth is peculiar in living documents ...

"The Body" With Emphasis on Heart

A Pediatric Intensive Care: Code Blue. Code Blue. Code Blue

A young male just coded. He could not be revived after considerable, intense medical interventions with the presiding, exhausted doctor herself taking turns at doing chest compressions. As usual, the team was large and diverse, as was the movement. Nursing, Critical Care Responders, Advocate, Chaplain, Organ Donation. Police.

Too many other deaths, too near on a timeline, and now this battered, abused child resulting in death was the precipitating, mitigating factor that took a young nurse down into a valley of great anger and sadness that needed place and space to feel and articulate.

"I can't take it." Her body, her voice, her choking tears were all convulsed and all tight. "Too many. This little boy beaten, beaten, beaten. I cannot stand the thought of it. Can you imagine? Who or what could do something like this to a child? No words for someone who could do this," as she shook her bent head. "I need to get myself together," as her voice trailed off. She continued to cry quietly, so I stood with her and held her, briefly encouraging her to take the time needed to feel her initial anger and pain.

After silence and feeling with her the tragedy of the night within the horrendous circumstances of this death: Together we prayed justice would prevail for Little Code Blue's perpetrators, so it would never happen again to another child in that family unit or any other.

"I'll be alright. I can work. Thanks for being here. I needed this." And I needed to hear that night as well that this Chaplain matters. I spent long minutes with her. She affirmed they were profitable minutes. It seemed good amid this heartache, that presence again counts, and it happens to be mine.

Reflection on Code Blue

We end where we began with an Emphasis on Heart. It was the literal physical heart of an incredibly young boy that stopped beating because of the cold hard-heartedness of those charged to love him. But a *heart*, more than one, did love and care for him in his final hours. His young, primary nurse's heart was anguished when his took flight, and she expressed for him the tears of outrage and the sobs of unspeakable injustices perpetrated on his innocence. He lives now only in her heart. She will continue serving him and so many others through nursing; it is in her heart.

The Doctor called, "Is a Chaplain in?" Her heart beats, too. She anticipated and she heard, and she responded, in trust of an interdisciplinary approach. The Doctor's heart continues on in my Chaplain's heart and whispers, there is hope between the medical and spiritual divides.

My heart: An occupied heart thinking of when bad meets good. Amid this night, we are team.

Different in discipline, yet same in heart: Sounds like Trinity.

Father, in the face of hardships and unspeakable human tragedies that unfold daily within the walls of hospitals, renew and refill the hearts of every clinical team member with your comfort, wisdom, and compassion. Dry their tears, take their weariness. Whisper in their ears, "Well done, my servants."

For the families, decimated by another's cruelty, may You grant them Your abiding love, sustaining strength, and unique courage as they navigate life in altered dimensions.

XI

ON A PERSONAL NOTE

XI

ON A PERSONAL NOTE

The following minis are a glance into my own personal journey, from my entrance into the Kingdom of God to a twice wrestle with the vocabulary of the medical disciplines, and a place of peace with the way I have walked in what I have known to be my God assignments.

The Human Condition ...

Before I came to Christ,
I lived in the World and For Myself ...

New Beginnings at 27

I lived in the world and For Myself

Truly, truly, I say to you, unless one is born again, he cannot see the kingdom of God. —John 3:3

*C*ircumstances: As my mother's life was seemingly slipping away, it reawakened in me the query of queries: What is it all about ... this thing called life? And so it was *in the facing of death that I found my life*. At the time, I was living in a small community nestled in the Adirondack Mountains of upstate New York. Nature became alive as never before: Sounds were distinct, and colors brilliant in a way that I had never known, although the gray of November was already beginning to settle in.

At the age of 27, I crossed the great divide between God and humanity as I surrendered my life to Jesus Christ while watching for the first time a Christian program called *The 700 Club*. I immediately experienced a profound peace and simultaneously wondered what *this phrase of being born again or born from above* would mean to me. Self-questioning began, and yet something undeniably happened and continues to this day.

The Journey is For A Life Time

Watchman Nee stated:

"Currently, the children of God who really seek after Him are divided into two classes: one class knows the Bible but knows little of God's power; the other does not know much of the Bible, yet knows the power of God. Very seldom are Christians well balanced in both points. It is not enough to just know the Bible, but that we must also know the power of God."

These comments continue to challenge me as they did when I first read them years ago. I have a heartfelt desire to be what Nee suggested is needed in the body of Christ today ... a person who is walking balanced in Word and deed. It is my hope that where I am privileged to minister, this balance is evidenced and that others will hunger for the same.

These past seasons in Christ have been filled with many personal and professional valleys and mountains, interspersed with mile after mile of flat lands and desert. It is now thirty-plus years since I responded to the love of God personally, but it is my continued testimony that Jesus Christ is faithful and true and that His plan offers *"a future and hope"* for those who will call on His name.

It is the "Author of Hope" for today, tomorrow, and into infinity Who set me free and keeps me free. I am, shall we say, no longer a victim of circumstances ... and you?

Like Timothy, I acknowledge the faith of those
who have gone before me.

May I Walk As Honorably
—PK

If You Must Define

*M*ore than. I am *more than* a survivor. For many years now, society has linked the word *survivor* with cancer. And I embraced it without much thought until as unexpectedly as a thief in the night, some rogue cells named cancer came knocking at my door. And at the moment of unquestionable medical evidence of the interloper's presence, I was a marked individual, joining the ranks of untold numbers who walk with me in time, as well as those who have gone before. Our journeys will not, cannot be the exact replicas emotionally, physically, socially, nor spiritually, just as our paths cannot be by design due to individual diagnoses, generally accepted treatment protocols, and more specifically, the underlying philosophies of both individual and medical team. Our known common denominator collectively remains our humanity, our conflict with fallen flesh. Truth, in simple terms, seems to state our outcomes of tomorrow remain mystery in our present day. Many live fully who were adjudicated dead by the voices of others. And others live by their own voices but as though dead.

If you must define ... then I choose to be known as an Overcomer.

The Story of Two Wolves

Author Unknown

An older Cherokee man is teaching his grandson about life. "A fight is going on inside me," he says to the boy. "It is a terrible fight, and it is between two wolves. One is evil. He is anger, envy, sorrow, regret, greed, selfishness, arrogance, self-pity, guilt, resentment, inferiority, lies, false pride, superiority, and ego. The other wolf is good. He is love, joy, peace, hope, serenity, humility, kindness, benevolence, empathy, generosity, truth, compassion, and faith. The same fight is going on inside you and inside of every other person." The grandson thinks about it for a minute and then asks his grandfather, "Which wolf will win?" The old Cherokee replies, "The one you feed."

In my present day of decision, I hear through the grandfather's voice a bidding to feed on the representation of that which is good. To me, the call is definitive. The choice is clear. I consciously choose to be an overcomer, not simply a survivor, in this season of trial wrestling with an unfathomable dark intruder. This invader has played an un-before-known dirge of pain in and on my body, and throughout a year sowed lyrics of defeat with sub-eerie notes in my mind-will. The ultimate intention was to weaken my spirit and redefine me and the essence of my personhood to something or someone other than one who is victorious, despite the voluminous mountain or deep desolate valley.

Which wolf will win? The wolf of faith, the good wolf of faith will win in me. If you must define, call me an Overcomer, whether I live or die today, tomorrow, or for a few or many more years to come.

*It is both my given and chosen inheritance in Christ
to be an overcomer.*

And you?

On Remission(ing)

*G*ood news! Good News! The results just in. Your scan is clean. Our protocols have been successful. The results: exactly what was intended. See you in three months for continued surveillance. And then the mantra repeats itself but the length between surveillance follow-ups ebbs and flows depending on findings. This is the world of medicine and the protocols of aftercare. To do less would violate the standards of excellence in medicine... and yet.

Transitioning

Cancer. Treatment. Survivor. Surveillance. And now Remission. Defined and painted once again in the language of another's tongue, medicine.

On the way to being Re-Missioned

In remission are the words that echo through the hallowed halls of medicine that cause most people to celebrate the pause. Yet, it does not resonate within me. This medical, *in remission*, knows no definitive time frame. It is unlike a musical score that is written with a mark that says, *Selah*, meaning a rest or pause in the music. The composer who writes the piece is the Master, who knows from the beginning where the pause will begin and end, unlike a doctor who manages a diagnosis. As creator he knows the end from the beginning, as does the living God.

When man records *in remission* for an unknown time quantity, God speaks. That is what I hear, although only a remnant will have ears to hear the call and respond. As though frozen in a time capsule of memories, memories and scars that whisper to them *life is no longer renewable,* they remain without the transforming element, the heat of hope. Missing body parts from surgery, or parts burned from radiation, and/or body parts retracted or weakened from lack of use are high and strong towers that will impede hearing and can stagnate effort.

Only God can penetrate the iceberg of fear. He alone says *live*. I have need of you in your refined state. Your *pause* by diagnosis now of remission, is in my holy sphere of omnipotence and omniscience. And I choose to re-define you today, to anoint you afresh, to *re-mission* you, and assign yet again a re-newed purpose. Seek me and you shall find your path.

Every day is a new day, and each day carries within it, seeds of hope and possibilities. The pause granted in a medical remission, the mark of Selah within a musical score, and the definitive rest in God's hands and time frame, all voice the same principle ...

Embrace your time. Live fully.

Peace As A Small Boat

*T*hat is me. I am as a small boat. And I have found a deep contentment in this truth. Metaphorically speaking, it seems I have been fashioned for waterways that take one to places, not unlike the by-ways of the highways, not the complex expansive interstate systems. I motor or paddle or sail to off-the-beaten-tracks often to the off-beaten people. Small places where God wants to send in a word, a phrase, a concept, a healing in which I was shaped to be a carrier. I am comfortable, perhaps, because I have found my forte. I seem only to hear and see, speak and write in the Spirit, in broad strokes. Principles. Rather sounds like a generalist in a specialist's world. The picture continues emerging. I am emerging, always emerging. It simply fits.

In The Hands of The Potter ...
transformation is a life-long journey.

EPILOGUE

No to Crusts and Crumbs

Job 42 (MSG)

ob answered God: "I'm convinced: You can do anything and every-thing. Nothing and no one can upset your plans. You asked, 'Who is this muddying the water, ignorantly confusing the issue, second-guessing my purposes?' I admit it. I was the one. I babbled on about things far beyond me, made small talk about wonders way over my head. You told me, 'Listen, and let me do the talking. Let me ask the questions. You give the answers.' I admit I once lived by rumors of you; now I have it all first-hand—from my own eyes and ears! I'm sorry—forgive me. I'll never do that again, I promise! I'll never again live on crusts of hearsay, crumbs of rumor."

> 1. Hearsay by law is defined as evidence given by a witness based on information received from others rather than personal knowledge.   2. Rumor is general talk without verification.

I will never again live on crusts of hearsay, crumbs of rumor.

It is not necessary. It is not advised. It speaks of deprivation. It may even prove to be detrimental. Living via the knowledge and experiences of others is living a secondhand existence. Besides, who, when there is a choice, deliberately chooses odds and ends, bits and pieces, snippets, or leftovers of others? Y*et, often, in the Spirit, this is exactly what many choose as a natural way of life—crusts and crumbs, hearsay and rumor.* And you? Whether young or seasoned, what is your operational level of life in the Spirit? Are you content to live and move and have your being fueled by someone else's definition or endorsement of God? Can you say from the depths of your soul that you are satisfied with your status quo, or does fulfillment or completion elude you? If the latter, there is hope. God's calling. Say yes to an ever-deepening personal relationship. It will not be a yes of futility, for as exercising in the natural pays dividends, so too does exercise in the spiritual realm.

No more to crusts and crumbs, hearsay and rumor as a way of existence concerning life in the Spirit. How do you want to be known by others, in the second or third persons?

God has always had more in mind for His people.

Reach, He Will Meet You There

Finally, I know and trust you will find, as I have found along the way, that God is beautifully faithful and true. I pray strength for your continued personal journey by the ever-present empowering of The Holy Spirit.

May the obedience of sharing my walk, entwined with the walks of others within the pages of *The Apron of Humility*, be found to be God honoring and a sweet aroma.

—PK

About the Author

"God has gifted her in a creative, powerful prophetic ministry to the Body of Christ and Church Leadership. It has been said that PK wields the Word of God like a sword, in a unique way, that God blesses profoundly with reconciliation and healing."

Rev. PK Price

PK PRICE is an ordained, non-denominational minister with many years of compassionate and rewarding human service and ministerial experiences across cultural, educational, religious, and social strata. She has worked with the homeless, victims of domestic violence, the intellectually-developmentally disabled, and the mentally ill, as well as families with youth at risk in clinical and community settings.

She is committed to calling all into higher pastures for life growth and maturation through preaching, teaching, and pastoral counseling by the administration of God's Word and the giftings of the Holy Spirit.

She has been privileged to minister in church, non-church, and conference venues in Africa, Asia, Europe, and the United States.

PK holds an AAS in Criminal Justice, a BS in Community Human Services, and an MA in Practical Theology from Regent University.

She currently resides in Western North Carolina.

PK is available for speaking engagements and can be contacted at:
ChaplainPKPrice@gmail.com

CPSIA information can be obtained
at www.ICGtesting.com
Printed in the USA
BVHW091347190522
637139BV00002B/5